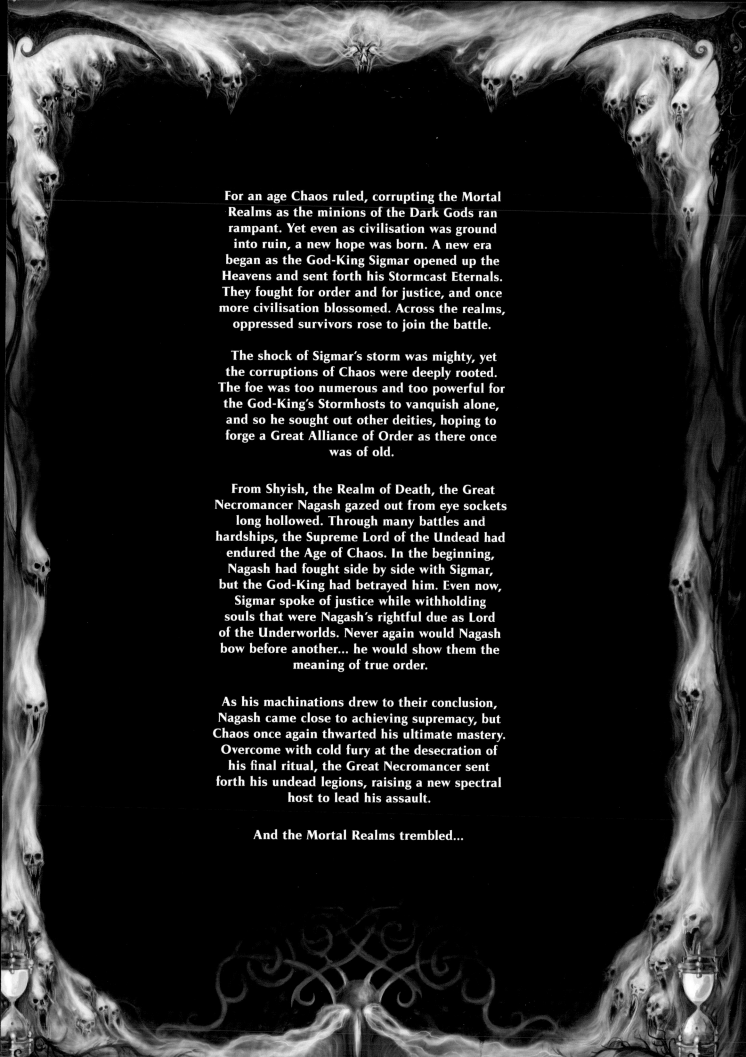

For an age Chaos ruled, corrupting the Mortal
Realms as the minions of the Dark Gods ran
rampant. Yet even as civilisation was ground
into ruin, a new hope was born. A new era
began as the God-King Sigmar opened up the
Heavens and sent forth his Stormcast Eternals.
They fought for order and for justice, and once
more civilisation blossomed. Across the realms,
oppressed survivors rose to join the battle.

The shock of Sigmar's storm was mighty, yet
the corruptions of Chaos were deeply rooted.
The foe was too numerous and too powerful for
the God-King's Stormhosts to vanquish alone,
and so he sought out other deities, hoping to
forge a Great Alliance of Order as there once
was of old.

From Shyish, the Realm of Death, the Great
Necromancer Nagash gazed out from eye sockets
long hollowed. Through many battles and
hardships, the Supreme Lord of the Undead had
endured the Age of Chaos. In the beginning,
Nagash had fought side by side with Sigmar,
but the God-King had betrayed him. Even now,
Sigmar spoke of justice while withholding
souls that were Nagash's rightful due as Lord
of the Underworlds. Never again would Nagash
bow before another... he would show them the
meaning of true order.

As his machinations drew to their conclusion,
Nagash came close to achieving supremacy, but
Chaos once again thwarted his ultimate mastery.
Overcome with cold fury at the desecration of
his final ritual, the Great Necromancer sent
forth his undead legions, raising a new spectral
host to lead his assault.

And the Mortal Realms trembled...

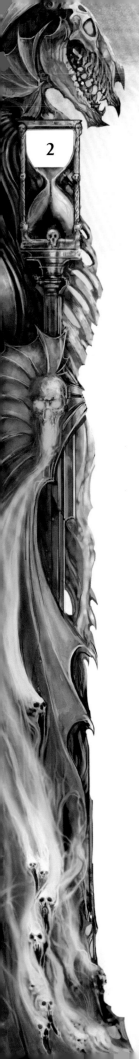

CONTENTS

DESIGNED BY GAMES WORKSHOP IN NOTTINGHAM
With thanks to The Faithful for their additional playtesting services.

Games Workshop Ltd., Willow Road, Lenton, Nottingham, NG7 2WS, United Kingdom
games-workshop.com

As dire omens predicted, the dead have risen in numbers beyond count. Lady Olynder, Mortarch of Grief, leads her Nighthaunt processions to bring doom and despair to the realms.

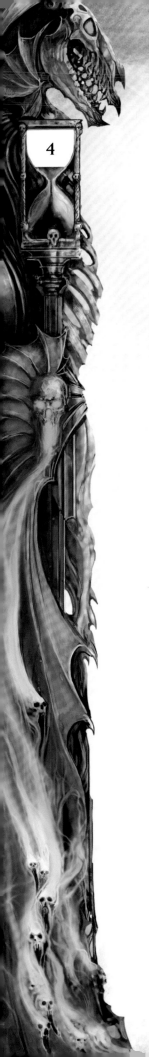

THAT WHICH HAUNTS THE NIGHT

An indomitable new malevolence has stirred an ancient terror. No longer content to hunt civilisation's edges, phantasmal forces gather into spectral armies. This is no mere haunting but a shock assault that seeks nothing less than to destroy life itself.

A fell wind is rising. From the darkest pits of Shyish, the Realm of Death, comes a storm of ethereal figures. An eerie mist spreads before them, blotting out the sun. They muster upon corpse-strewn battlefields or ancient burial grounds, a ghostly army of phantoms. They are the supernatural, the dead, the damned – the Nighthaunts.

Sustained by a fathomless hatred for the living, these wraiths fight to send fresh souls screaming down into the darkened realms from whence the dead emerged, taking cruel pleasure in knowing the torments that await their victims below.

And by the manner of their death shall ye know them…

MALIGNANT SPIRITS

The Nighthaunts are the horrors that haunt the periphery, terrors that prowl beyond life's edge. They wait with the patience of the eternal, yet their hunger drives them with insatiable needs – to hunt, to harm, to destroy life – for that is all that is left to them. They come in many forms, but all are destined to forever stalk the Mortal Realms and to drag the living to the same doom.

The Nighthaunts have not only lost their lives, but also their physical bodies. While mortal flesh rots away, the spirit lives, taking on a new, phantasmal aspect. Whatever blissful underworld rest or eternal peace that was promised to these souls has turned out to be naught but lies. Instead,

Nighthaunts are fated with afterlives of damnation, stripped of any compassion they had before death. All warmth is eradicated, leaving behind only the negative. What remains of their spirit is bitter, hate-filled and bound by necromancy, often in some cruelly ironic way linked to either their deaths or their deeds in life. They must forever haunt the Mortal Realms, to seek out and punish those who dare to still live.

Glowing with a fell light, the Nighthaunts are a bone-chilling sight. They appear nebulous and insubstantial, able to hover weightlessly in the air or pass through solid obstacles. A Nighthaunt can glide without pause straight through a wall as a man might stride unimpeded through light fog. Unless guided by supreme faith, enemy blades and arrows pass harmlessly through the Nighthaunts' incorporeal forms.

Only those that can steel their minds and drive out their deepest fears can stand against such supernatural horrors. It takes unstinting courage to will a weapon to pierce a phantasm. In return, the chill blades of

the Nighthaunts reap a deadly toll upon the living. Skeletal hands reach out, ignoring armour, flesh and bone alike to grasp at a foe's heart. The fear and confusion that emanates from each of the unholy gheists robs enemies of their physical strength just as it saps their conviction.

Though almost impervious to physical harm, Nighthaunts carry with them their own hell. Some are cursed by the dark manner of their death. For instance, those who met their ends in chains might have hoped to escape their captivity in the afterlife, yet in the spiritual world are bound by more manacles than ever. Others find their deeds in life turned against them – a mortal who spent a lifetime healing and nurturing might find that, as a spirit, they can only wantonly destroy. Such morbid rewards fill the Nighthaunts with rage and hatred.

The perpetrator of these eternal torments is none other than Nagash, god of the underworlds, the Great Necromancer, the Supreme Lord of the Undead and self-proclaimed ruler of Shyish. Nagash finds the twisted irony he has inflicted to be naught but poetic justice. His vindictive nature, limitless spite and unfathomable ego have created the most terrible of spirits, gheists and wraiths.

A single Nighthaunt might terrorise a village, and a pair acting together could leave an entire fiefdom quaking in fear. When gathered en masse and united beneath a greater undead spirit, such an army can destroy an empire, and become the stuff of dire legends.

THE PROCESSIONS

Nighthaunt armies are known as processions. Fear runs before them as tangible as the unnatural mist that rises from the ground. The air grows chill and then, from out of nowhere they come, riding on the wind. They surge over the land like a phantasmal tide.

Some of the wraithly host ride upon spectral steeds, their hooves never touching the earth but leaving footprints of cold fire in the skies. Horrible lurching shapes hover, moving in disjointed fashion, but travelling terribly fast for all that. There are rank after rank of ethereal crook-backed things, cowled creatures brandishing tall glaives. Others come in chains, rattling and moaning. Ghastly apparitions leer from tattered hoods, spectral scythes sweep forward, while mind-splitting howls and harrowing shrieks echo through the gloom.

Many foes flee at the first sight of a Nighthaunt procession. Others hold their ground for a time, but it does not take long before senses sharpened by fear begin to make out sinuous shapes moving in the thickening fog. Panicking defenders leap at every new swirl – and they are right to. Clawed talons reach out, phantom riders appear out of the sinister vapours, and spirits

materialise from unexpected quarters, drifting through trees or over untraversable moats.

The Nighthaunt onslaught is not merely a physical assault, but a psychological one as well, and only the bravest dare to stand before them.

RISING THREAT

Once, Nighthaunts were the stuff of myths and fables. Tales told of specific hauntings, such as the Bloody-handed Baron that stalked the ruins of Fornorn castle, or spine-chilling events like the return of the Shrill Sisters, who came back to massacre the village that burnt them as witches. Every region of the Mortal Realms could boast bloodcurdling tales or gheist-

frequented sites. In addition to these lone revenants, Nighthaunts could also be seen bound to the service of a Necromancer or Soulblight vampire, but most stalked the lands of the living purely under their own malevolence. That was before cataclysmic events in Shyish opened up a nightmare. Nighthaunts flooded the Mortal Realms, rising up unexpectedly to strike fear in the hearts of all mortal creatures. Seeing the effectiveness of these sudden shock attacks, Nagash organised a new wing of his legions. The Nighthaunts would be his outriders of horror, the first wave for his long-planned Soul Wars. To command this new vanguard of terror, Nagash appointed a new leader – Lady Olynder, Mortarch of Grief.

With amazement, the guards of Griffon Tower watched one of their brethren stagger out of the forest. Opening the shim-field portcullis they raced out to aid the injured warrior, who by his armour and markings was part of the Vanguard-Hunter retinue that had been on patrol to the north. His body-plate was unrent, but his helm was missing, and his haggard face told a tale of agony and terror. Struggling against those who sought to hold him up, the Stormcast seemed not to recognise them at first. Then, his wide eyes appeared to focus and he struggled to say something, but for minutes no words came.

'They are coming!' he spoke at last, his face conveying pure horror. And then, his final message delivered, he could hold on no longer and was gone. His body shifted to azure light, a beam that blinked up to the heavens, leaving no trace.

'I have never seen a foe cause such fear in one of us,' said Metallus. 'What could it be?' The question stood unanswered. As one the Liberators returned to the gatehouse with many glances cast towards the black forest behind them.

'Whatever is coming,' said Liberator-Prime Augustus, 'they will find they can't get past us and the walls of Griffon Tower.' As the enchanted portcullis shut behind them a chill wind swept from the north, the air itself seeming to moan in protest. A mist rose, impossibly fast, its unnatural green-tinged swirls seeming to hide ominous shapes. A horn of Azyr sounded and from the top tower came the staccato reports of the longstrike crossbows opening fire.

Even as the Liberators peered out into the fog the foe was upon them – charging through the walls came cowled spectres brandishing gleaming scythes. Grinning skeletal apparitions wreathed in balefire were the last things the Stormcast Eternals saw, before they vanished back to Sigmaron to be remade anew. Soon, no defenders stood between the Nighthaunts and the townships beyond the tower's walls.

From out of the rising fog comes a deathly procession of Shyish. They are the riders in the dark, the takers of souls, the Nighthaunts. By the time the wraiths emerge from the mist it is too late – too late for protective rhymes, too late for the sign of the Hammer. All is macabre, all is death. Ask not for whom the reaper comes – he comes for thee.

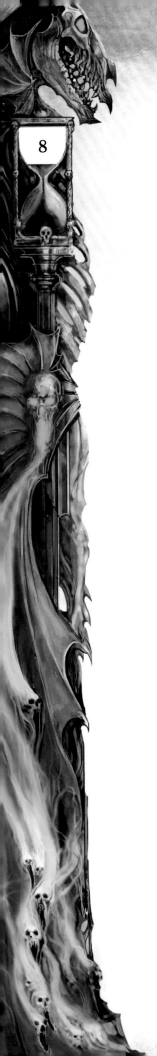

THE RESTLESS DEAD

There are many different types of undead, and there is much speculation amongst those learned in the arcane arts about such entities and their maker. As necromancy is a dark and often forbidden subject, few mortals know the true extent of its rituals, and it is often fatal to learn too much.

Across the Mortal Realms the dead do not rest easy. Unquiet spirits haunt and terrorise the living, re-animated cadavers rise from their graves at the bidding of Necromancers, and immortal Soulblight vampires plot nefarious schemes of conquest while draining mortal blood for sustenance. A dread figure casts a long shadow over all – Nagash, father of necromancy, god of the underworlds, and ruler supreme of all undead.

HATRED OF LIFE

Nighthaunt spirits are many and varied, but all have one thing in common – a hatred of the living. Some, like the Cairn Wraiths, were as wicked in life as they are in death – all but their most vile traits have eroded away, their hate still clinging to them and driving them onwards. Others, like the Glaivewraith Stalkers and Chainrasps, are embittered by the curse of their afterlife, for now they are yoked to an eternity of torment and their jealousy of the living is boundless. They are goaded to destroy all that still draws breath – some are even mistakenly convinced that doing so will earn them a reprieve. Yet such is not the nature of Nagash. For a few spirits, like the Dreadscythe Harridans, the hatred is integral to their curse, for they cannot control themselves and must watch helplessly the horrors they are compelled to commit.

UNDEATH

Those that dare to study the forbidden arts of death magic – curious wizards, wayward apprentices and would-be Necromancers – generally accept that there are three main ways to create undead. The first and most common of these is the enslavement of the deceased's remains – the necro-evocus. Zombies and skeletons – worm-eaten corpses and desiccated bones – can be reinvigorated through necromantic incantations. There is no life or personality in such risen creatures, merely dark magic that binds their bodies to a will greater than their own.

The second way in which undead are created is the necro-procratus – undead making more undead. The simplest version of this is the bite of a zombie, which can infect the stricken so that upon their death they too rise up. There are several variations of necro-procratus, some involving organised ritual.

The third method of creating undead is the most complex – the necro-maledictus. This takes the form of a powerful eldritch curse cast upon a soul that has been recently separated from its physical body. These hexes can vary by region and culture throughout the Mortal Realms, but in all cases they consign a terrible fate upon the spirit. Instead of passing onwards into the underworlds, the afflicted spirit will instead remain on the mortal plane, doomed to haunt it for eternity.

The scholars of the Collegiate Arcane widely believe that all necromantic magic originated from Nagash and the mortific spells he devised. However, there are instances of natural phenomena, such as drifting pockets of amethyst magic or particularly rich veins of grave-sand, leading to the creation of Nighthaunts as well.

Souls become so twisted by death magic that they take ominous new forms, becoming ghostly killers intent on destroying the living. There are many varieties of Nighthaunt, with hundreds of different maledictions creating distinct phantasmal beings, some of which are believed to be unique in nature. The great majority of Nighthaunts, however, fall into one of about a dozen broad categories – specific types of wraiths such as the spiritually imprisoned Chainrasp Hordes, the cursed healers known as Dreadscythe Harridans, or the mass-grave amalgamations known as Spirit Hosts.

There is a twisted and dramatic irony to the fates of those souls cursed to become Nighthaunts. One who lost their family and their own life to base betrayal might be cursed to an afterlife where they unflinchingly serve the killer that took everything from them. A criminal bound in chains that came to long for his life to end so that he might know freedom may find his spirit self still weighed down with stocks and manacles for evermore.

It is Nagash that is behind these cruelties. He is unforgiving to a degree mortalkind cannot fathom. However, he does not mete out punishments out of the boredom of eternity, nor does he play with souls for his own amusement, for such concepts are anathema

to the Great Necromancer. To Nagash's cold yet orderly mind, the macabre penances to which the Nighthaunts are subjected are but justice, for there is not a single mote of mercy within his being. To the God of Death, mortals that attempt to escape fate or thwart his designs deserve the very harshest of dooms.

Over the centuries Nagash has invented many different curses to punish deserving souls that enter the underworlds. Some of these powerful hexes linger in perpetuity, lurking in the underworlds like spiders, waiting for similarly marked souls so that they might latch onto them as well.

THE THORNY BRIAR

Thorny briar is a plant commonly associated with undead, and with the Nighthaunts in particular. Its barbs represent the spirits' eternal pain and the cruelty of their existence, whilst the grave roses that sometimes appear on its stems further denote death, tragedy and bleakness. The vine's creepers endlessly curl into knots, allegorical of the inescapable plight of these revenant spirits and the hopelessness of their fate, for although the necromantic forces holding Nighthaunts together can be broken by sorcery, or violence driven by sufficient willpower, over time their shattered essence reforms in the underworlds of Shyish and they return to their morbid un-life. There are few weapons or spells in the Mortal Realms powerful enough to destroy a Nighthaunt once and for all.

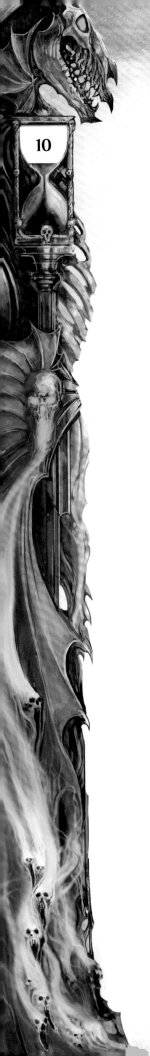

SOMETHING WICKED THIS WAY COMES

The Mortal Realms have always been stalked by the spirits of the dead, but they are now flooded with Nighthaunt creatures like never before. This is the unintended result of a plot that has been under way since the realms were young. Thus is born a new era of terror…

In all the realms there have always been hauntings – the scratching at the shuttered window, the creaking opening of latched doors, the mysterious light that beckons from the swamp. These phenomena are caused by lesser gheists, the shadows of spirits, and the residual ill will of vengeful mortals that have passed on to the afterlife. Yet there are other, far more powerful spirits from beyond.

Those entities known as Nighthaunts are undead that possess far greater animus and influence than troublesome poltergheists or apparitions of mourning. Nighthaunts come back from the dead not to antagonise, lament or memorialise, but to vent their anger – to kill the living and to send their souls screaming back to the same eternal torments to which they themselves are subject.

Throughout the ages, some Nighthaunts have become creatures of dread and legend, and the living tell many tales of their hauntings. Some of these creatures – such as Cairn Wraiths and Tomb Banshees – would occasionally be discovered by Necromancers or Soulblight vampires. These powerful undead bound into servitude such Nighthaunts, harnessing and directing the spectres' destructive tendencies for their own ends.

On rare occasions, like the unholy anniversaries of great cataclysms or intense influxes of amethyst magic, entire Nighthaunt hosts would arise. Whole towns were known to have disappeared before

the wrath of these ethereal armies, but luckily such supernatural eruptions were few and far between. At least, that was the case before the Shyish necroquake.

PLAN OF AGES

Nagash's plans for domination began when he awoke during the time known as the Age of Myth. It was then that the Great Necromancer first claimed Shyish, yet it was not only the underworlds of the Realm of Death that the god coveted.

Nagash's plan for ultimate supremacy was a subtle one, and required an immense amount of time, magical power and tireless labour – all things the Great Necromancer held in abundance. To harness the necessary arcane energies, Nagash sought out grave-sand – the realmstone of Shyish that was solidified death magic in its purest form.

As with each of the realms, magical energy was not evenly spread throughout the lands of Shyish, but rather could be found in far greater quantity and quality at the Realm's Edge. Thus, in Shyish, the greatest abundance of grave-sand was found heaped in dunes along the very periphery of its domains. It is commonly

believed that each mortal creature has their own stream of grave-sand, and that, so long as its grains trickle down the dunes, their life will continue. Should that sandstream fail, however, the mortal life is likewise ended. Those who might attempt to travel to that region of Shyish to ensure a continuous flow of sand put themselves in dire peril, for there amethyst magic waxes so strong that hurricanes of baleful power sweep the dunes, destroying any living thing that dares to intrude.

While a mortal creature could not last long beneath the lashing ending-power of so much concentrated amethyst magic, the same cannot be said for the undead. Nagash sent his minions – endless lines of skeletons – into the dunes to collect the precious resource. They proved able to survive the trek into those forlorn territories, but still, each could only carry a single speck of realmstone, for even they could not stand indefinitely against such arcane might.

Over many centuries, countless skeletal figures made the journey, relentlessly marching to retrieve their one grain of grave-sand before returning. It was a journey of countless thousands of leagues, and many were lost, crumbling to dust beneath the magical barrage, waylaid by skaven raiders, or beset by any number of the terminus creatures – the dreadful undead beasts that stalk those regions. Others simply continued to trudge, then crawl, until their limbs were ground down to nothing and they could move no more.

As the centuries rolled by, Nagash amassed a vast store of grave-sand. Mountains of the realmstone were used to construct a monumental masterwork – an echo of the Black Pyramid of the world-that-was. Yet this pyramid was built inverted, held aloft by complex spells of binding. Its tip hovered but a hand's span above the ground, and it soared upwards to a towering height.

Warning signs of the vast accumulation of death magic were perceived by those attuned to the arcane. Malign portents caused armies from across the Mortal Realms and the Realm of Chaos to be mustered against Nagash's growing power. Shyish was invaded from hundreds of points. With the pyramid's construction nearing completion, the many battles fought to waylay the Lord of Undeath at last took a toll – the skaven unwittingly disrupted the orderly workings of Nagash's arcane edifice, resulting in a cataclysmic shift. The inverted pyramid began to spin, and the flow of amethyst magic in Shyish was altered, drawn from the Realm's Edge to the epicentre of the vast monument.

THE NECROQUAKE

The explosion of magic that ensued was beyond even Nagash's abilities to control. A mind-splitting wave of eldritch power shook the Mortal Realms and ripped at the very fabric that tied them together. A wave of death magic washed over the cosmos. In each realm, spectres and fell spirits long dormant were roused to vengeful action, attacking with no plan other than to sink their dagger-like talons into the living. Billions of dead souls rose up anew, assailing anything that still breathed with a hatred beyond comprehension.

This was the necroquake of Shyish and it altered the Mortal Realms forever.

In Shyish, the Great Black Pyramid absorbed so much amethyst magic it began to sink, buckling the underworlds in a whirlpool of downwards-pulling energies. So was the Shyish Nadir born, drawing all souls towards it. Not even Nagash could master its energies.

While his plans to fill himself with enough arcane power to conquer the Mortal Realms had gone awry, Nagash had flooded everywhere with the undead. On a grand scale the Great Necromancer saw the full might of wraith hosts unleashed, and the terror they caused. There were more such spirits roaming the lands than ever, although their attacks were more instinctive than planned. But that would soon change…

SYMBOLS OF DEATH

Even the greatest of mortals eventually falls, like autumnal leaves, to mix with the dirt below. Throughout the different cultures of the Mortal Realms there are many symbols associated with death, such as the purple grave rose, the gnarlyew tree, the thorny – sometimes bleeding – briar thistle, the reaper's scythe, the mourner's veil, the dully sheening Morrcoin and the flickering corpse candle, to name a few. These images are rife with meaning and magical potential, and many superstitions revolve around them. In Shyish, the symbols of death take on even greater significance, for they are powerful conduits of amethyst magic.

Perhaps the most potent of all deathly symbols is the hourglass. With its sands slipping from one chamber to another, the hourglass is used to mark the passage of time, and is an obvious reminder of mortality. The stream of sand runs steadily, so that at a casual glance its movement seems almost imperceptible, yet gradually the sands drain. Strangely the stream always seems to run most swiftly towards the end. Those most knowledgeable in necromancy often use the hourglass in disturbing rites and rituals, often using its powers to sustain the unnatural state of undeath itself. When filled with grave-sand and imbued with dark powers from the retronovis ritual – a powerful incantation of reversal – an hourglass can reinvigorate the necromantic magic that binds the undead. A powerful enough version of the spell can even have strange temporal effects, slowing the foe down to a nightmarish crawl from which they cannot escape, or even aging them in rapid fashion.

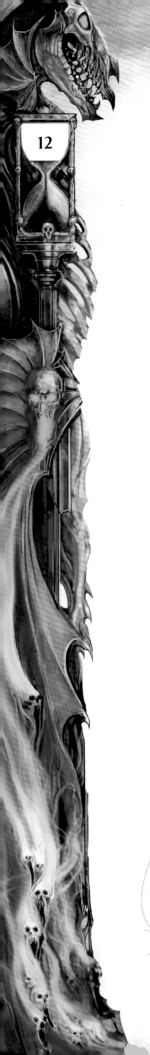

THE RISE OF THE WRAITHS

During the necroquake of Shyish, Nagash witnessed the terror sown by the profusion of malignant gheist hordes. Here was the perfect shock attack – a terrible psychological weapon to unleash into the very heart of his mortal foes.

Although the Nighthaunt attacks during the necroquake had wreaked havoc, there was much to be improved upon. The assaults often dwindled, targets of opportunity were poorly chosen, and there had been little or no coordination between the different phantasmal armies. In the free city of the Phoenicium the spectral hosts had all but defeated the defending garrison of Stormcast Eternals, but then became sidetracked, content to terrify the populace rather than razing the city. The Sylvaneth defending their wooded fortress of Gnarlok were conquered, but none of the gheists sought to claim the highly magical woadstone that the children of Alarielle guarded, leaving it to fall

into the hands of Beastmen. Two successive waves of Nighthaunts washed over the Stormcast defences guarding Vandium, each nearly defeating the foe, but had they attacked as one the undead would have easily triumphed. From the Kharadron sky-port of Barak-Zon to the hidden undersea cities of the Idoneth Deepkin, many places were ravaged by the rampaging spirits, but there was no concentrated effort to finish off the mortals.

To address such shortcomings, Nagash sought a commander, a leader that would unite and drive the Nighthaunts to not just terrorise mortalkind, but to devastate them, leaving the shocked survivors ripe for Nagash's final crusade.

THE SEARCH FOR A NEW MORTARCH

The Mortarchs are Nagash's top lieutenants – powerful undead leaders that have been granted a sliver of the Great Necromancer's power. Each of the existing Mortarchs, of which there were three, was chosen for their unique skills. Should Nagash need corruption he would turn to Neferata, Mortarch of Blood. If he needed to make a gory example of the foe, then he would call upon Mannfred von Carstein, Mortarch of Night. For the most secretive missions and empire-building, he favoured Arkhan the Black, Mortarch of Sacrament. All commanded their own undead legions and all wished to wield still more power. Yet Nagash desired a

new element, and also loyalty, for of the Mortarchs only Arkhan the Black was truly content to serve.

The tale of how Nagash scoured the underworlds for a new subordinate is a long one, for there are untold dominions of the dead. From Stygxx, the Land of Forgotten Gods, to the hidden cold-fire plains of Helstrom; from the relic-filled lands of Carstinia to Hallost, Land of Dead Heroes, no afterlife was left unsearched. Nagash fixed his baleful gaze upon many souls – champions of unconquerable tribes, tyrant-kings of long-forsaken empires, matriarchs of bloodthirsty sisterhoods. Yet Nagash sought some quality they did not possess.

It was not clever manipulation, base cunning, or well-planned military strategy that earned the armies of the dead so many triumphs during the necroquake – it was shock and terror. The most overwhelming victories had been won through the suddenness of their assaults and the wave of fear that spread before the invasions and hung heavily over all lands through which the spectral hosts passed. Nagash was impressed with the psychological effect of the Nighthaunt armies upon the fragile and superstitious minds of mortals.

In truth, Nagash had forgotten the notion of fear, for it had been ages since he had felt its tremble. Despite his supreme intellect, the Great Necromancer, in his long plans, had allowed his logical mind to strategise without factoring in the emotions of mortals. It was a rare mistake, and one he vowed not to repeat.

In all his travels across the underworlds, Nagash found none like the Veiled Lady. Here was a spectre he had punished many centuries ago with a unique curse. In life she had

been Lady Olynder, a beauty famed throughout the empire of Dolorum – the largest of civilisations from the lands known since the Age of Chaos as the Screaming Wastes. She had schemed, plotted and used charm to climb socially, leaving behind a trail of ruined suitors and deaths under mysterious circumstances. So great was her appeal that she wound her way upwards, winning the hearts of nobles and then, eventually, the Dolorum prince himself. Her betrothal to the future king ended on the very night when the prince and his father, the high king, disappeared. In their absence, she became the ruler of Dolorum.

Vowing to mourn her missing prince and king, the young queen took to wearing a veil. Her people called her the Mourning Bride or the Unrequited Queen, and her public display of grief won over even the coldest of hearts. Yet it was all a lie – her shows of remorse were false, her sorrows no more than a ruse. Hidden behind her veil and deceitful sobs, she could not help but smile at her own cleverness.

Elsewhere in the realms the travails of the Age of Chaos had begun turning civilisations into ruin, although Dolorum had thus far been spared. That came to an end when the plague arrived. Soon the queen's sorrows were for her realm, but again, all her tears

were false. She was safe in her palace, and her life a dream, even as all those around her died in the agonised throes of a weeping pox.

Through it all Nagash had watched the empire of Dolorum, for its people had always honoured him. Their dedications had ended with the crowning of the new queen. Even when her lands, cities and throne room were all but empty of life, Lady Olynder felt no real grief, and she attempted to parley with the agents of Nurgle. It was then that Nagash claimed her soul as his own. So did Olynder become the Veiled Lady, a spectre burdened to feel all the miseries of the Mortal Realms and forced to haunt the ruins of Dolorum. After the passing of many centuries, during which Nagash gave not a single thought to her fate, the god was surprised at what he found when he discovered her once more.

The Veiled Lady had again risen to rule over old Dolorum, although it had become a land swarming with wraiths and spectres. During the upheavals of the necroquake, Olynder subjugated the phantasmal denizens that arose there, drawing them closer with her spreading aura of grief. So haunted were the lands that any living being that dared enter them experienced true terror. Yet rule of one underworld could not satisfy her ambition, and the Veiled Lady longed to bring more nations – living and dead alike – beneath her dominion.

Here, at last, was the leader that Nagash was looking for, and so in dark ritual the Great Necromancer granted Lady Olynder a sliver of his own divinity. He knighted her the Mortarch of Grief, and tasked his new lieutenant first with uniting the Nighthaunts, and then leading them as the vanguard of his new crusade.

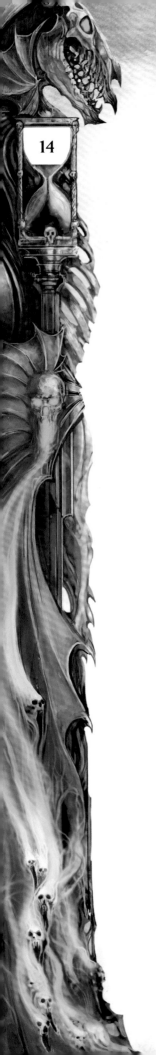

REIGN OF TERROR

Untold spirits were invigorated during the necroquake, blasted forth to wreak havoc on a tide of amethyst magic. Subsequent aftershocks sent out further ripples of phantasmal destruction. The spectral armies spent themselves haphazardly, breaking off into splinters to terrorise many mortals before ultimately disbanding, returning to local sites where there was a rich deposit of death magic.

Yet it was not long thereafter that the spectres heard a summoning, a siren call that not even the strongest-willed spirit could resist. This was not the imperious summons of Nagash or his harsh lieutenants of old, but a new voice. It was an unholy lamentation, a call that was at once a soulful wail that bemoaned the half-life horrors of a wraith, but also a promise of vengeance – a vow of black-handed revenge upon all who still lived.

With all realms still suffused with amethyst magic, the dead stirred once more, though this time not to attack, but to return to Shyish.

At Nagashizzar, it was Lady Olynder who summoned the Nighthaunts. She divided the massed undead into armies and appointed sub-commanders, assigning a Knight of Shrouds to lead each spectral host. As was her wont, all this was conducted in a morbidly ceremonial fashion – in ghostly processions. Not until the next wave of aftershocks emanated from the Shyish Nadir did Lady Olynder unleash her newly assembled forces.

Like the howling of an ill wind, the spectral hosts advanced on a hundred fronts. They would strike first in Shyish, and then move through Realmgates to spread terror across the other realms. The old empire of Lyria was the first to feel the wrath of Lady Olynder's

new Nighthaunt processions. Relentlessly they moved from one target to the next.

A NEW WAY OF WAR

With sudden and terrible swiftness the Nighthaunts attacked. In many locations the horizon turned an eerie greenish-blue – an ominous spectacle caused by the oncoming wave of vengeful spectres. Elsewhere they dove down from night skies, rose from ground mists, or swept straight through protective walls.

In Lyria, upon the Plains of Narth, were sprawled the armies of the eight-armed Chaos warlord Thur. It was beneath his iron fist that several underworlds had been ransacked, and countless souls claimed for the Dark Gods. Now they were encamped on the plains, and only a week's march from the cairn-city of Glymmsforge.

In an attack characteristic of dozens of others across Lyria and hundreds more over the expanse of Shyish, three Nighthaunt processions turned the campsite into a bloodbath.

Bypassing all pickets and guardians, the Nighthaunts emerged from below. Surprise was complete, and in moments all was bedlam as panicking foes routed. A thousand different melees erupted between the bonfires as hordes of chain-wrapped spectres rose up to overrun hulking Dragon Ogors. Frenzy met its own as Gorechosen clashed with scythe-armed wraiths, neither side willing to take a step backwards in their eagerness to slaughter the other.

So devastating was the Nighthaunts' assault that the battle was over in moments. But the wraithhosts did not haunt the battlefield. Instead, they disappeared, already en route to their next target.

Those foes who dared to stand against the quick-strike attacks led by the Mortarch of Grief found themselves embroiled in a rapidly moving campaign like no other. They fought against armies that did not need food or rest and that left no physical sign of their passage, leaving foes to speculate where or when the wraiths might arise again.

Nighthaunt processions used their ethereal nature to full advantage. Entire armies rose out of the ground to strike without warning, and disappeared just as quickly. In the rare instances when their assaults did not work as planned, their armies simply melted away, sinking into the earth or stepping into eerie mists to disappear entirely.

The Nighthaunts' targets found themselves ground down, worn out from fighting and chasing phantoms who were not beholden to the same

worldly limitations as they. But worse than any physical strain was the psychological onslaught. Even the bravest might tremble before the wail of a Tomb Banshee, or startle at the sudden appearance of the spectres. But there was something more.

Surging like a bow wave before the Nighthaunt processions came an overwhelming sense of fear, dread and foreboding. This was the effect of Lady Olynder, for misery flew about her like wind around the eye of a hurricane. As enemy commanders sought to rally their troops they found even their most stalwart regiments moving more slowly, crushed under the oppressive weight of their own hopelessness.

Many victories followed – during the Siege of Morlaix, Lady Olynder herself destroyed the Lord-Celestant in command of the Stormcast foe. At the Third Battle of Traitor's Gulch, a procession under Baron Morbosi secured the Calcified Realmgate, and at the Mausoleum Mountains a force of Nighthaunts reclaimed their underworld of old, driving off the Sigmarite interlopers. But not all battles were triumphs.

At Glymmsforge, the Anvils of the Heldenhammer held off the Nighthaunts long enough to allow some of the most hated Stormhosts to once more escape the Great Necromancer's vengeance. The final battle to reclaim all of Lyria was fought at Ghrun. There, Lord Thur summoned the Bloodthirster Khazkhan, leader of the Helfire Legion.

The Chaos forces broke Lady Olynder's Grimguard and nearly succeeded in destroying the Mortarch. Only the arrival of Arkhan the Black and Nagash himself turned the tide, and saw the foe vanquished.

Although pleased with her conquests, Nagash judged Lady Olynder to be overly headstrong. To censure his newest Mortarch, Nagash orchestrated another of his cruel ironies. She who used betrothal only to climb to power was forced into marriage with a would-be king who was every bit as ambitious as she. Nagash deemed the indomitable spectre of Kurdoss Valentian a suitable match. He would provide brute force and tactical advice to complement Olynder's supernatural might. Yet Kurdoss would never rule. It had been his all-consuming ambition in life to command, though now that he had finally risen to sovereignty, true authority was forever denied to him. Together they would serve Nagash, aiding him in ushering in a new age – the Age of Undeath. The Soul Wars had begun.

THE SOUL WARS
Nagash lays claim to Shyish and every soul that enters the underworlds – an entitlement he believes was agreed upon by the gods of Sigmar's Pantheon long ago. Though some, like the Chaos Gods, challenge this claim openly and are known foes, those members of the Great Alliance, along with their followers, who withhold souls from this destiny are branded traitors. And many have been so denounced – from Sigmar and his Stormcast Eternals, to the aelven races, the Sylvaneth and more – and it is Nagash's plan to make them pay.

SHYISH, THE REALM OF DEATH

Shyish is a realm of endings, where amethyst magic is strongest. Within the realm's borders are every underworld ever summoned into being by the beliefs of mortal cultures. At the centre of all stands the great citadel of Nagashizzar, where the Supreme Lord of the Undead dwells.

Throughout the ages the civilisations of the Mortal Realms have each forged mythical concepts of where the spirit departs to after death. All of these imagined afterlives coalesce in Shyish, the Realm of Death, shaped by common ideologies and given form in that realm by its abundance of amethyst magic. Yet the realm is not solely the domain of the dead, for in addition to the many lands therein that are utterly inimical to life, there are those which are entirely habitable by the living.

Shyish is a series of sprawling landscapes and oceans with a deep pit in the centre – the Shyish Nadir. Much like a whirlpool, this central vortex draws in those things that are near to it, though it operates on not gravity, but amethyst magic. Since the necroquake, those underworlds that are forsaken or forgotten by their mortal believers, or have simply run their course, are dragged closer to the Nadir. There they are swallowed, crushed

to ultimate nothingness, for above all else Shyish is a realm of endings. As civilisations decline and disappear, as empires crumble, eventually so too do their underworlds.

Yet whether an underworld is populated by the living, the dead or both, all are haunted places. Amethyst magic is plentiful and veins of grave-sand marble the lands. When the mists rise it is said that they can re-animate corpses or lure those cursed souls that have become Nighthaunts. The underworlds themselves are magnets for the eldritch energies of ending, and they shape many environments, flora and fauna that would be impossible elsewhere.

All of the living inhabitants of Shyish – from feral tribes to civilised city-folk – have devised their own wards against the restless dead. It is often said that mortals from Shyish are highly superstitious, and this is true, for each sect has developed their own

methods of warding off the many revenants that prey upon the living. For them this is a simple necessity that must be learned by any mortals daring to live in a realm of underworlds and afterlives.

'Never have I seen such bleak landscapes, such forlorn vistas. It is a grim place for grim folk, and for the dead, for everywhere there can be found spirits.'
– Anaximander, cartographer of Azyrheim

CONQUERED BY CHAOS

During the Age of Chaos, Shyish came under assault by the Dark Gods and their minions. Many of its lands were overrun, both those settled by mortals and areas populated solely by spirits. Cities were levelled, the greatest cairn-monuments were cast down, and the hungering Chaos Gods devoured souls while their armies planted foul icons wherever they conquered.

Even Nagash was beaten, forced to retreat and recover. For centuries he was trapped, the armies of the Dark Gods besieging the underworld he had taken refuge in. Despite their best efforts, the forces of Chaos could not gain access to Nagash's sanctuary, for travel between the underworlds can be notoriously difficult without a deep understanding of necromancy.

THE DEAD RETURN

The Great Necromancer was not destroyed, merely biding his time. Whether by happenstance or design, he timed his return with Sigmar's reopening of Azyr and the Stormcast Eternal assaults upon the Mortal Realms.

With the coming of the so-called Age of Sigmar, Nagash and his Mortarchs launched dozens of campaigns to drive back the forces of the Chaos. In the Prime Innerlands, in places like Charnelcourt and the isle of Dhûmi, the undead rose up and re-conquered their lands entirely, cleansing them of the threat of Chaos.

And then came the near completion of Nagash's great plan, and the necroquake. This cataclysmic event altered the lands, changing the polarity of the flow of death magic in Shyish and stirring the undead to new heights of activity across all the Mortal Realms.

With the labour of millions of undead, the great capital of Nagashizzar was rebuilt so that once more Nagash could ascend his throne. Now fuelled by the power of the Great Black Pyramid, Shyish draws in all souls so that none might escape Nagash. Yet the Nadir is so incredibly rich in amethyst magic that even Nagash can not dwell there indefinitely. It is a place of insanity as well as death, and even the most ancient of vampires and liches feel the compacted nothingness of pure endings crushing down upon them in that deathscape of changeless eternity. It is from this epicentre of pulse-less power that Nagash launches his endless streams of invasions – both to reclaim the rest of his realm and outwards to punish the Mortal Realms.

Despite the many victories achieved by Nagash and his Mortarchs in the Realm of Death, the vile tendrils of Chaos still run deep in a great many places. Areas like Gothizzar are still controlled by Chaos, as are the grim forests of Modrhavn and the entirety of the Kraniad Isle. Ossia is in a constant state of desperate war, even as it is slowly dragged towards the Shyish Nadir. Some of the most corrupted regions – like the tainted Rictus Realmgate in Grishlon or the Bone Gardens of Omeghar – are held by daemon legions.

WELLSPRINGS OF TERROR

While all of Shyish is suffused with dark energies, and Nighthaunts can be found in every underworld, there are some sites of unholy power notorious for producing spiritual horrors. The Wraithfjords, to the north of Carstinia, the city of Muertzhan and the isle of Honour's End have each produced scores of Nighthaunt processions. The nation of Vinculus is home to the single largest Chainrasp horde to ever haunt the Mortal Realms – in life, its inhabitants rebelled against the rule of Nagash, and so he cursed each and every one of them to be linked for eternity by arcane shackles. Yet wherever a spirit originally hails from, all now rush to heed the siren call of Lady Olynder.

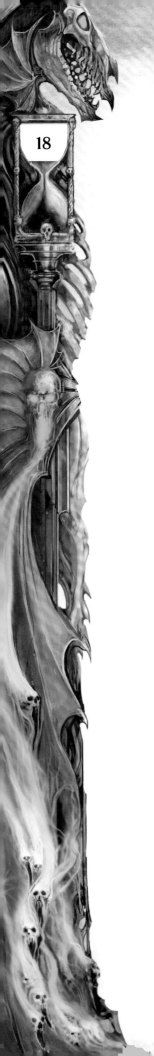

CHRONICLES OF TERROR

To the ageless spectres of the Nighthaunts time is immaterial, its passing all but meaningless to those that live a phantasmal existence of eternal ending. Here are chronicled the pivotal deeds of the Nighthaunts throughout each of the major eras.

● AGE OF MYTH ●

There is a great deal of Nighthaunt activity during these years, but entire armies composed of Nighthaunts are rare occurrences.

RULER OF THE DEAD

Early in this period, Nagash claims rule over Shyish and constructs his great citadel and seat of power, Nagashizzar. He charges his Mortarchs with enacting his will across the realm.

THE TIME OF NEW BEGINNINGS

During the alliance between Sigmar and Nagash, dozens of cities are founded across Shyish. In some – such as Gothizzar, Glymmsforge, Mortistan and Sepulchtan – their mortal citizens either pledge themselves to Nagash or sponsor a Cult of Death that earns the Great Necromancer's favour. In others, such as Shadespire or Hawthorne's End, their lack of proper respect for Nagash spells their ultimate doom. Such is the nature of Shyish, for it is a place of endings far more than new beginnings.

● AGE OF CHAOS ●

Occasional, small-scale incursions into Shyish by the followers of the Dark Gods give way to full-fledged invasions.

SOULSTORM

At the Battle of Dirge Peak the undead suffer great losses and are unable to withstand the massed onslaught of Bloodletters led by the Bloodthirster Khazkhan. Khorne had ever coveted the lands of fallen heroes in the Realm of Death, and wished to claim them as his own.

In desperation, Nagash rips forth the souls of a thousand mortal prisoners, using them to fuel a great summoning. In response, the spirits of the entire underworld of Nordyrie – a northerly section of the Endless Boneyard in Hallost – answer the call. In life they were all once heroes, but had put down their swords claiming they would fight only for a cause, never for pay. In death, Nagash's curse had made them ruthless mercenaries, who would combat any foe if their price in souls was met. The ethereal host not only halts the daemons' advance, but defeats them utterly. Only Khazkhan escapes destruction. The Nordyrie become the first entirely Nighthaunt host to be mustered for a specific purpose, and their services are destined be called upon many times.

FALL OF DOLORUM

Once the largest of Shyish's civilisations, the empire of Dolorum falls during the Age of Chaos. The last ruler of those lands, Lady Olynder, is cursed upon her death by Nagash so that her spectre feels all the sorrows of the realms.

THE GREAT BETRAYALS

The members of Sigmar's Pantheon become increasingly estranged and divided. Nagash finds evidence that Sigmar is withholding souls from the underworlds. At the Battle of Burning Skies the promised undead aid does not arrive, and Sigmar blames his ensuing defeat upon Nagash, abruptly ending their alliance. Even amidst the multiple Chaos invasions across all Mortal Realms there are battles between former allies, as the forces of Order feud amongst themselves.

CHAINWRAITHS

The Idoneth Deepkin of the Mor'phann enclave raid all along the borders of the Great Quagmire. In their quest for souls they enter the Vale of Chains, accidentally releasing a spectral host that was cursed by Nagash to be tormented there for eternity. Freed from their bondage, the Chainwraiths seek to kill the living, but also take their revenge upon any undead that serve Nagash.

THE FALSE KING

Kurdoss Valentian almost succeeds in usurping the crown of Khajhi, but his coup is short-lived. Valentian's backstabbing draws Nagash's ire, so that upon his death the craven king receives a powerful curse…

RUINATION

At the height of multiple Chaos invasions, Nagash attempts to counter-attack. At the culmination of the War of Bones he is defeated by Archaon, and his physical form is shattered. While Nagash slowly reforms in the safety of a hidden underworld, the Chaos forces level cities, desecrate cairns, and even sack Nagashizzar. Amidst the ruins are raised the dread symbols of the Dark Gods. During this time of Chaos supremacy, only the Nighthaunts are effective in fighting the minions of the Ruinous Powers, for even the Mortarchs have slunk into hiding. Several Nighthaunt forces grow in notoriety during this time, including the Glowing Host – a strangely luminescent horde from the Glittering Marsh boasting no fewer than twelve Tomb Banshees – and the embittered Grimguard, outcasts from the now Chaos-controlled city of Gothizzar.

● AGE OF SIGMAR ●

Even as Sigmar unleashes his Stormcast Eternals a resurgent Nagash bursts forth from the Starless Gates. He summons a tempest of amethyst magic, raising his legions and launching hundreds of attacks to drive off the Chaos invaders.

BATTLE OF OSSIA

Stormcast Eternals arrive throughout Shyish, and the battles in Ossia are particularly fierce. As the undead rise up, alliances are formed between the two estranged factions. The fighting wavers back and forth, but with the arrival of the Mortarchs the Chaos strongholds are eventually cast down. Nagash does not forgive those of Ossia for allowing themselves to be conquered.

THE RETURN OF ORDER

Spurred on by Sigmar and his Stormcast Eternals, the forces of Order seize many pivotal Realmgates. It is not long before these beachheads are expanded into fortresses, and then rapidly grow into cities as free peoples flock to burgeoning civilisations.

MALIGN PORTENTS

Deities and wizards skilled in the arts of augery read malign portents in the air. Nagash's long plan of domination is at last detected and many armies rush into Shyish to halt the Great Necromancer.

NECROQUAKE

Employing assaults designed to delay his enemies, Nagash nearly succeeds in fending off those who would invade Shyish and wreck his plan. However, skaven agents contaminate the Great Black Pyramid. The resulting necroquake sends massive waves of necromantic energies across the cosmos, and leads to the creation of the Shyish Nadir.

A QUEEN SHALL RISE

After a long search that saw Nagash peer into every underworld known to him, the Great Necromancer selects Lady Olynder and appoints her as his Mortarch of Grief.

BATTLEFIELD SHYISH

Lady Olynder's first task is to begin the long task of driving back the Chaos forces that still dominate Shyish. Over one hundred Nighthaunt processions are hurled into the fray, fighting alongside Nagash's legions. Each of the existing Mortarchs sees the opportunity to take Lady Olynder's measure. Although Mannfred von Carstein and Neferata resent the newcomer's share of power, all of the Mortarchs quickly realise she is a formidable addition to their ranks.

CLOUD RAIDERS

An enterprising sky-fleet of Kharadron Overlords attempts to build a base from which to plunder the aether-gold that drift high above Shyish. Their ability to remain above the clouds had kept them safe from many foes – but not Baroness Ravenblack and her Blackguard procession. The duardin are swept over by packs of Dreadscythe Harridans. One by one, the guns of the Kharadron fall silent, and their ships plummet from the sky.

BRIEF ALLIANCE

In many places the newly anointed Nighthaunt processions join forces with Flesh-eater Courts in order to destroy Chaos invaders. Such alliances are of convenience only. At the Battles of Lake Lethis, the Grymfens, and throughout the campaign of Ossia the tale was the same – after the common foe was defeated the spectral hosts turned upon the vile cannibals and destroyed them also.

THE BRIAR QUEEN

The Briar Queen – nemesis of the cursed city of Shadespire – is unleashed by Nagash to menace other lands. She is tasked with claiming certain souls that have cheated Nagash. With the aid of her spectral army – the Thorns of the Briar Queen – she visits each of the Mortal Realms, always bringing back her target's soul. Between missions the Briar Queen returns to Shadespire, for her need for vengeance there remains unsatisfied.

NEAR DISASTER AT GHRUN

The last battle to cleanse Lyria of Chaos is almost Lady Olynder's undoing. Although victorious in the end, her near destruction at the hands of a Bloodthirster draws censure from Nagash, who both punishes and rewards his new Mortarch with her betrothal to the Craven King, Kurdoss Valentian.

THE SOUL WARS

Nagash deems it is time to launch his long-planned crusade to reclaim all those souls he sees as rightfully his – that is, all souls that ever were. Strikes are levelled against the factions that have betrayed Nagash by withholding the spirit-stuff of their dead – the followers of Chaos, the Stormcast Eternals, the Idoneth Deepkin, the aelves of Hysh, the Sylvaneth and the Daughters of Khaine among them. The first wave is conducted by the Nighthaunt processions. Thus, even in the wake of the necroquake, a further tide of undead attacks sweeps across the Mortal Realms. Led by the Mortarch of Grief, every major free city is assailed. The Nighthaunts prove themselves beyond doubt to be the tip of Nagash's spear of terror.

THE GRIMHAILER

During the Nighthaunt attacks, none are more active than Reikenor. Time after time, the Grimhailer uses the shock of his spectral assaults to crush his enemies utterly, claiming many souls for Nagash.

GHOSTLY PROCESSIONS

For battle, the spectral hosts of wraith creatures are organised by order of Nagash. Beneath the overall command of Lady Olynder, the Mortarch of Grief, the Nighthaunt processions are sent forth to wreak havoc as the vanguard of the Great Necromancer's deathly forces.

Nighthaunts have always been wayward spirits, prone to following their own thirst for revenge. Only when ensnared by a more powerful being – such as Nagash, a Mortarch, Soulblight vampire or Necromancer – do the ethereal creatures submit to following another's lead. But now, even the most isolated have been enthralled to Lady Olynder, the Mortarch of Grief.

At her summons the spectres muster, answering a siren call that promises vengeance against the living. Lady Olynder organises the massed phantasmal hordes, breaking them down into hard-striking and distinct armies.

On the most vital campaigns, Lady Olynder leads her own Nighthaunt procession, often accompanied by her spectral consort, Kurdoss Valentian. More frequently, however, a procession is commanded by a Knight of Shrouds. There are notable exceptions, as powerful spirits are sometimes given generalship over a wraith host. Infamous examples of such individuals are Reikenor the Grimhailer and the Cairnking Angrimm, both of whom are often known to command their own armies. Although Kurdoss Valentian is sometimes sent on missions away from Lady Olynder's side, he is never the commander – another of Nagash's cruel ironies.

A Nighthaunt procession draws much of its character from its commander. For instance, the most rage-filled or bloody-handed of generals invigorate their minions and charge forward in quick-strike fashion. More gloom-ridden doombringers prefer to pin the foe in place, eroding their will with waves of desolation before hurling in elite reserve forces to finally break the enemy.

Beneath a procession's commander are any number of captains – Dreadblade Harrows, Spirit Torments, Cairn Wraiths, Lord Executioners, Tomb Banshees and Guardians of Souls. These potent spirits are used to lead

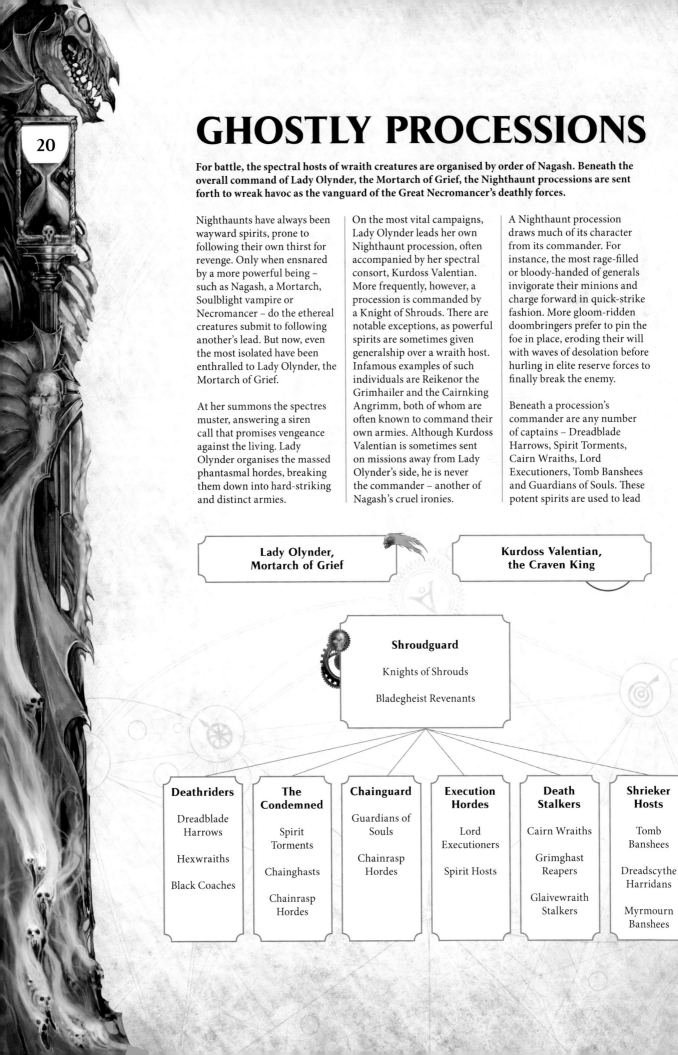

Lady Olynder, Mortarch of Grief

Kurdoss Valentian, the Craven King

Shroudguard

Knights of Shrouds

Bladegheist Revenants

Deathriders	**The Condemned**	**Chainguard**	**Execution Hordes**	**Death Stalkers**	**Shrieker Hosts**
Dreadblade Harrows	Spirit Torments	Guardians of Souls	Lord Executioners	Cairn Wraiths	Tomb Banshees
Hexwraiths	Chainghasts	Chainrasp Hordes	Spirit Hosts	Grimghast Reapers	Dreadscythe Harridans
Black Coaches	Chainrasp Hordes			Glaivewraith Stalkers	Myrmourn Banshees

assaults or to unleash potent attacks upon the foe. A few such spectres have achieved notoriety, such as the Briar Queen of Shadespire, and the Knight of Shrouds Sir Morwyrt Blackheart, who is always accompanied by a trio of Lord Executioners. Some commanders use their captains as bodyguards, while others prefer a Shroudguard – a circle of Bladegheist Revenants bound by magical oaths to protect their liege at all costs.

The bulk of most Nighthaunt processions are drawn from the ethereal rank and file – less powerful but more numerous spirits like Chainrasps and Glaivewraith Stalkers. These are grouped together and are typically led by one of the wraith captains. Such formations have different strengths, and are usually deployed with specific purposes in mind by their commanders.

A Chainguard comprises large numbers of Chainrasps under the control of a Guardian of Souls. These hosts are often used as the centre of a Nighthaunt battleline, or for holding up powerful enemies. Even as the Chainrasps are destroyed, the Guardian of Souls uses its magic to reform them, creating an anvil upon which many foes break. Other groupings of Nighthaunts include the Death Stalkers – hunting forces tasked with seeking out and destroying particular enemies – and the Condemned – Chainrasps and Chainghasts driven mercilessly into the enemy by a Spirit Torment. Such ragged multitudes are less concerned with holding up the foe, more with slaying them.

Other Nighthaunt formations are fewer in number but made up of more powerful spirits. The Shrieker Host is such a gathering. Led by a Tomb Banshee, it is composed of Dreadscythe Harridans and Myrmourn Banshees. Ideally, such a force drifts towards the battlefront while the enemy is engaged. Just as the Tomb Banshee unleashes her hellish shriek, the Dreadscythe Harridans sweep in to unleash their fury. The Myrmourn Banshees devour enemy spells while adding their own chill daggers to the fray. Few foes survive the charge of a Shrieker Host, but those that do soon find their will to fight failing beneath its horrible cacophony.

When spectral cavalry ride to battle alongside a Black Coach, they are collectively known as Deathriders. These fast-moving contingents are ideal for smashing apart the flanks of the enemy army and for launching sudden attacks. An Execution Horde, meanwhile, concentrates a great deal of power into a compact force. Its constituent Spirit Hosts and the Lord Executioner that leads them are able to manoeuvre between larger formations before closing in to deliver the killing blow.

As per Nagash's command, Lady Olynder sends forth her processions as quickly as she forms them. Those that meet with success are given new tasks by the Mortarch, while those that fail are summoned back to Nagashizzar. There, the merciless Lady Olynder breaks the spectral host apart and reassigns its various spirits to different armies, resulting in a variety of compositions between the processions. Some remain homogeneous, for they are formed from spirits gathered from the same locale, like the hoarfrost-covered wraiths from Helspoint that glow with a cold light, or the Blood Mavens – a force dominated by Dreadscythe Harridans known for their crimson locks. Other processions are more disparate, each battalion or unit drawn from different underworlds, or even from other realms.

Under the rule of Lady Olynder, and driven by her fierce demand for victory, many processions have already garnered a fell reputation. The strangely lambent Glowing Host from the Glittering Marsh field an inordinate number of Tomb Banshees, and have proved unstoppable in their many attacks upon the Chaos forces in Shyish. The vast Chainguard host from the fallen lands of Viniculum do not simply defeat enemy armies, they overrun entire populations. The Reaverhost hail from martial stock, for they come from the underworld reserved for the finest knights of old Dolorum. It is said when the moonlight strikes them at the right angle, a pale and ghostly hint of the livery they wore in life can still be seen.

Sana knew the end was near. Every rasping breath she drew pained her. As the village healer, she had done all she could with her knowledge of herbs to ease the agony of her passing. Now, there was nothing to do but wait. And Sana was ready – she had outlived her husband and her frail form no longer worked as it used to. She hoped to soon be reunited with her love, for such was the belief of her people – that the worthy would be gifted an afterlife with other goodly souls. She knew nothing about Nagash's curse on healers. When next she opened her eyes all the warmth of the world was gone. She now floated like mist, her hands replaced with reaping scythes. In a dreamlike state Sana watched her new, horrible form commit the worst atrocities, a rage beyond her control driving her to attack all that still lived.

LADY OLYNDER, MORTARCH OF GRIEF

Nagash sought everywhere for a commander to lead his newly risen Nighthaunts, and found none more terrible than Lady Olynder of Dolorum. As the newly appointed Mortarch of Grief, it is she that rules the spiritual hosts that seek to establish a reign of terror across the Mortal Realms.

She is the Mourning Bride, the Unrequited Queen, the Veiled Lady and the Mortarch of Grief. She is despair made manifest, gloom given form. She is Lady Olynder, and in her are bound all the sorrows and anguishes of the realms.

Each of Nagash's Mortarchs has been anointed with a portion of the Great Necromancer's vast power. To Lady Olynder, who feigned sorrow in life, he gifted a mantle of misery – she now felt all the woes of the Mortal Realms, becoming a weaponisation of grief itself. Her power transcends the melancholic, for she exudes mind-crippling waves of purest desolation. Mortals in her presence are overwhelmed by a gloom so heavy that only the strongest willed can remain upright. Most fall to their knees, mentally battered by their own utter hopelessness. It is a sorrow and regret potent enough to cause a mother to forsake her child, a warrior to lay down his sword and accept the inevitable, to stop a beating heart.

Lady Olynder hovers above the ground, attended by her bridesmaids, a pair of banshee handmaidens. As she advances, the thorny vines of grave-roses instantaneously sprout before her, their flowers rapidly blooming and dying in order to lay a path of fallen petals beneath her floating form. In her hands the Veiled Lady wields the Staff of Midnight, an ornate stave topped with a polished gemstone of vitrified grave-sand. The lightest touch of this staff is enough to wither a mighty oak, or kill a grown man outright. Yet it is not Lady Olynder's deadliest weapon.

In addition to being surrounded by an aura of absolute misery, Lady Olynder is also a powerful sorceress. With her incantations, she can direct a pall of despair to weigh upon her foes, slowing them like some unholy lodestone. Those afflicted suffer a

mental burden so dire it causes even the bravest to tremble, their martial prowess lessened by leaden limbs and despondency beyond any hope of redemption.

In the midst of this bleak atmosphere she has created, Olynder presses forward, her banshee bridesmaids shrieking a wail of the damned while slashing with spectral talons at foes who draw close. One bridesmaid bears an ensorcelled grave-sand hourglass – a gift from Nagash – that can be smashed asunder with lethal effect. Yet Lady Olynder has another, even deadlier weapon. From behind her thin shroud, the sunken eyes of

the Mortarch of Grief fixate upon a foe. Deliberately she pivots to face them, before slowly and solemnly lifting her veil. What horrors they see are unknown, for none have yet lived to tell the tale. So does Lady Olynder conquer, leading the fore of Nagash's invasion in order to bring a new age of eternal death over the Mortal Realms.

'Do not resist – death is inevitable. The more quickly you succumb, the sooner your suffering will be over. Come to me, and be mine for evermore...'
- Lady Olynder

KURDOSS VALENTIAN, THE CRAVEN KING

The dire presence of Kurdoss Valentian is announced by dirgeful trumpets and grim proclamations of his basest deeds. The Craven King sits silent and motionless upon his drifting throne until he closes with the enemy, and then he wields the Sepulchral Sceptre to deadly effect, mercilessly slaying all whom his queen bids.

Nagash needed an appropriate lieutenant to serve his newly crowned Mortarch of Grief. Kurdoss Valentian proved an especially fitting choice – the king provided Lady Olynder with a fearsome bodyguard and a tactically minded advisor, and their cold betrothal was cruelly pleasing to Nagash.

In life Kurdoss had a ruthless desire to rule, and many were his wicked deeds to claim power, including the assassination of allies, the betrayal of entire armies and the murder of his own brothers. Just as Kurdoss took up the fallen crown of his last sibling, Nagash claimed his soul. Unlike his brothers, Kurdoss did not worship Nagash, but instead had chosen the God-King Sigmar as his patron – reason enough to draw the Great Necromancer's ire.

Even as a wraith in the spirit world Kurdoss' relentless ambition saw him rise. Nagash was impressed with the Craven King's resourcefulness and fighting skill, yet it was not his desire to see Kurdoss claim rule over an underworld nation. The Great Necromancer whisked Kurdoss away from the afterlife kingdom he was usurping for his own, instead granting him a touch from Alakanash, the Staff of Power. In doing so, Nagash bestowed upon Kurdoss great might, yet also an accompanying curse.

Nagash ensured that Kurdoss' ultimate dream of rule was realised in name only, for he was betrothed to Lady Olynder, fated to always follow her lead. Indeed, Kurdoss became little more than a strongman – a bitter jest to be so close to all he desired, yet still so far away.

Kurdoss bears several symbols of his new office, including the throne he aspired to sit in life. He also carries the Sepulchral Sceptre – a weapon that in Kurdoss' hands can split rock or crack open a gargant's skull.

Kurdoss utters not a word as he hovers upon his throne. Only when he wishes to smite the foe does he deign to move from his despondent posture. The same cannot be said for his spectral attendants. These are the spirits of two who Kurdoss betrayed and supplanted as part of his bloody path to commandeer rule. Now the heralds are fated to serve him eternally and announce his many triumphs. However, they take cruel glee in declaring his defamatory titles – the Usurper, False Lord and Craven King – and interjecting with boasts of the many ignoble deeds that marked his quest for power.

Once forceful and commanding, Kurdoss Valentian's curse prevents him from speaking in anything more than a whisper – gone are his days of booming orders and taking charge. When prudent, he issues tactical advice garnered from his many victories upon the field of battle, but when he attempts to say more, nothing but the dust of ages issues from his mouth. An aura of bitterness exudes from Kurdoss so powerful that it can choke enemy captains and generals even as they seek to issue their own orders, the words foundering and dying upon their trembling lips.

REIKENOR THE GRIMHAILER

Once a sorcerer-king rich in the knowledge of amethyst magic, Reikenor ran afoul of Nagash. Now, in undeath, the Grimhailer is cursed to serve the Great Necromancer, acting as his chief reaper of souls. There are few sights more ominous than the macabre wraith-wizard atop his winged steed, lit by the eerie light of his corpse candles.

In Shyish, Reikenor is known by many names – the Grimhailer, the Reaper-wraith and the Storm Rider among them. Sorcerer, master of terror, reaper of souls, fell lieutenant of Nagash – Reikenor is all these things and more.

Much of Reikenor's origins are mysterious, lost to time, but what is known is that he was once a learned sorcerer-king who sought to overcome death. Through the magic of Hysh – harnessing the very light of reason – Reikenor worked towards preventing all mortality. His quest for knowledge on the subject was all-consuming, and he attracted many acolytes and followers. Eventually Reikenor's attempts to unbind the workings of death drew the ire of Nagash himself.

In the afterlife the Grimhailer still hunts, but now he does so in the name of Nagash. His quarry is no longer eldritch secrets of mortality – instead he seeks those who transgress against his master. Through his arcane powers Reikenor can sense those that withhold souls from Nagash, tamper with his necromantic rituals, desecrate his monuments or commit any other sacrilegious act. Those who are not in service to Nagash but pursue necromantic knowledge are especially targeted.

Upon detecting blasphemies, Reikenor swoops down upon his winged steed shrieking the syllables of powerful hexes whilst dealing sweeping blows with his scythe, Fellreaper. However, even those Reikenor slays in battle he is not finished with – for such unfortunates he has further torments in store.

Through his incantations, Reikenor can summon a wraithstorm – a cyclone of amethyst magic that stirs those souls recently separated from their bodies. Inspired by Nagash's desire to see grim justice meted out upon those that offer him insult or rebel against his wishes, Reikenor's spell incites the departed spirits to savagely attack their former comrades. The spell creates a spectral hurricane in which wraith-like phantoms hack and pull down the living. Thus is a dark vengeance delivered to those that would thwart Nagash.

To aid Reikenor in his appointed task, Nagash has bound to him Kyllaron, a fierce winged Nightmare. Mounted on the undead steed's head armour are a grim assortment of corpse candles. They are a unique mix of tallow rendered from Reikenor's former apprentices along with a grave-sand mix. Indeed, after his soul was claimed by Nagash, it was the Grimhailer's own disciples that were his first target. They too were blasphemers and Nagash deemed their fate fitting. By snuffing out the flame of a corpse candle, Reikenor can end the life of a nearby mortal or siphon off a portion of his own essence – either way, by doing so he creates a surge of arcane force to empower his enchantments. The Grimhailer is now condemned to kill forever, and that he must extinguish light and create darkness to do so is a cruel twist that Nagash holds as one of his most just punishments.

Prior to the Shyish necroquake, Reikenor often hunted the Mortal Realms on his own. Following the rise of Lady Olynder, the wraith-wizard has joined the Nighthaunts, leading processions on her behalf or following missions set by the Mortarch of Grief. So is his power greater than ever before.

KNIGHTS OF SHROUDS

Born of tragedy and betrayal, Knights of Shrouds are spectral commanders blessed with unholy power by Nagash himself. They are the leaders of the Nighthaunt armies, the directing minds behind the processions of horrors that serve the Great Necromancer. Where these fell generals lead, terror soon follows.

In life, Knights of Shrouds were military commanders – great leaders of men that bartered their souls away to Nagash. In return, these spirits have been granted power and immortality, becoming generals in command of the Nighthaunt processions.

The making of a Knight of Shrouds does not occur at random, for Nagash does nothing on impulse. Since the Age of Myth the greatest champions of mankind were targeted, and whether they led unruly hordes or disciplined armies full of pomp and pageantry, undead hosts were thrown against them. Some of those warrior-exemplars died in combat, others rallied their troops in order to stave off disaster. However, time and numbers have always been on the side of the dead, for Nagash is immortal, and his armies legion.

Over time, no few of the opposing leaders were ground down. Only those that were willing to betray their own people and pledge an oath to Nagash were spared. These traitors were granted immortality, transformed into spectral generals. Many have been held long in hidden underworlds, yet only now has Nagash unleashed them to lead his Nighthaunt processions.

Even the most cold-hearted Knight of Shrouds suffers some degree of anguish over their betrayal, and in order to forget their past each plunges headlong into their duties and the blackness of undeath. Each tells themselves they had no choice, that anyone else would have done the same in their position, but a worm of doubt forever gnaws at what is left of their soul. They are cursed to forever carry their misdeeds, and also to bring death to the living.

Upon forfeiting their life to Nagash, a Knight of Shrouds is gifted a Sword of Stolen Hours – a cursed blade that steals the soul energy of those it slays, transferring a portion of that power back into its wielder. As they did before their spectral existence, some Knights of Shrouds ride to battle upon ethereal steeds, while others prefer to fight on foot. All are formidable bladesmen – fell-handed foes with many lifetimes' worth of battle experience.

It is not solely for their martial prowess that Knights of Shrouds are appointed as Nighthaunt commanders, however. These were leaders of soldiers, canny generals that understood the arts of war. Now, their chill, disembodied voices ring out over the battlefield, directing their forces and instilling them with a fierce vigour not seen in the unliving hosts of the Deathrattle and Deadwalkers. While the Nighthaunts automatically heed a Knight of Shrouds' orders, the living consider these dire figures to be the worst kind of traitors imaginable.

DREADBLADE HARROWS

The Dreadblade Harrows are the officers beneath the Knights of Shrouds. In life, each of these wights watched their leader's betrayal, neither helping nor hindering. Their half measures have been duly rewarded with a curse in death, for they are compelled to serve their treacherous lords eternally.

Even for Nighthaunts, Dreadblade Harrows are especially discorporate, phantasmal figures atop spectral steeds, who can disappear and reappear at will. They are the Knights of Regret, full of bitter recriminations. In battle they serve as bodyguards and lieutenants, or are despatched as outriders. Rearing upon their spectral steeds, they vanish into wisps of mist only to gallop out of thin air elsewhere to fulfil even the most unchivalrous commands – culling the vulnerable, cutting off retreating warriors, and other heinous tasks.

SPIRIT TORMENTS & CHAINGHASTS

Immortal and vindictive, Nagash created Spirit Torments and Chainghasts to capture and watch over unrepentant offenders and – perhaps most importantly of all – to persecute them. Here are the gaolers of Shyish, the Keepers of the Keys and the fell guardians of the underworlds.

SPIRIT TORMENTS

The Spirit Torments are the lords of the Great Oubliette of Shyish, a continent-sized underworld of dank cells and ice-cold dungeons. Known as shacklegheists to the elders of the Shyish Innerlands, they were once a rare sight in the Mortal Realms, but following the eruption of fell magic during the necroquake they have become far more common. Since the launching of the great processions the Spirit Torments have regularly joined the Nighthaunt forces.

Spirit Torments are entrusted with a duty Nagash considers vitally important, for it is their role to capture the souls of transgressors – in particular those that Nagash sees as having escaped their due fate. For this reason, Nighthaunt processions that are tasked with the hunting and capture of specific souls are always joined by Spirit Torments.

A Spirit Torment draws its victim's soul into its shacklegheist chains – heavy bonds forged of malefic iron and tempered by fell ritual. This chill metal acts as an enchanted jail, trammelling the life-force as soon as the attached lock closes tight. The spiritual energies cannot escape until the padlock is re-opened, an act that is typically done upon the procession's return to its haunting grounds in Shyish. There, the heavy arcane vessels are unlocked, delivering their contents into the clutches of a gaoler king, or perhaps a Mortarch.

The fate of a Torment-apprehended spirit depends upon the strength of the soul and the crimes that it committed in its mortal life. The majority are remade into lesser Nighthaunts, but some are instead trapped in a pocket of unreality linked to the Great Oubliette. A very few are instead reserved for some exquisite misery dreamed up by the ever-vengeful Mortarchs, or even Nagash himself.

While a Spirit Torment can collect any drifting soul that has been recently severed from its physical body, the cruel nature of the spectral gaolers means that they far prefer to be the agent of the separation themselves. With a groaning effort the Spirit Torment hoists up the jangling chains and begins to swing them. The heavy, lock-capped links whirl with impressive momentum, and should one connect, it will stave in a ribcage or a skull as easily as a direct hit from a cannonball.

Spirit Torments take pleasure in their dark work, though as much as they delight in ending lives and capturing souls, there is one aspect of their duties they enjoy above all others. The spiteful phantoms can peer into their padlocked prisons, gazing over the bright soul-stuff captured within. Then, they draw a great breath with a discordant howl, a chilling inhalation that steals hope, robbing the imprisoned spirits of energy even as it subjects them to nightmarish angst and dread.

Filled with the energies of the incarcerated souls, the Spirit Torments exude an aura of malevolence and despair. At times this malignant force can even be seen as pale, greenish wisps of spiritual radiance amongst which faces leer, taloned hands reach out to grasp, and agonised screams echo. To the living these emanations evoke purest terror, and are oppressive even to those who cannot see. To bask in such baleful phenomena is to be overcome with feelings of morbidity and gloom. To other Nighthaunts these harrowing energies are invigorating, driving the wraith-creatures on towards still greater acts of violence and spite.

There are many Spirit Torments, but some have earned great infamy. Karceris the Black-hearted was the gaoler of the Gristlespine tribes during the Chaos conquest of Morthaven. His misdeeds became legend, but near his end Karceris disavowed his past, attempting to cleanse his soul with penitent acts. It was not enough, and Nagash claimed him, naming him the phantasmal overseer of the Cryptopolis – the largest of the dungeons of Nagashizzar. Other Spirit Torments, such as Mawcrasp of Malendrek's procession or the Rusthaunt of the Crimson Procession, have earned their fell notoriety for the sheer number of souls they have returned to the great mausoleums of Nagash.

The Spirit Torments have been more active and seen further abroad since the coming of the Shyish Nadir, but they are rarely seen alone. They are accompanied by wraith-like enforcers and lackeys, the most common of which are the manacle-laden Chainghasts.

TO CAGE LIGHTNING

There are some – from Shyishan scholars to the astromancers of Azyrheim – who believe there is a correlation between the appearance of Spirit Torments and the Stormcast Eternals. Whether sheer coincidence, or symptomatic of cunningly laid traps, the appearance of Sigmar's Stormhosts – especially in Shyish, but also in other realms – draws an inordinate number of Nighthaunt processions containing one or more Spirit Torments. On battlefields where the two sides meet in open warfare, there have been multiple sightings of the soul-capturing wraiths using the power of their shacklegheist chains to prevent the typical return to the heavens of the slain Stormcasts. Surely, Nagash seeks to reclaim souls he sees as rightfully belonging to him.

CHAINGHASTS

Chained captives awaiting a terrible doom are wont to plead, beg and call out for divine aid. However, Nagash is a god without the slightest hint of mercy. To the Great Necromancer it matters not whether those iron-bound prisoners are guilty or innocent, or if their ends came swift or were cruelly prolonged. He cares only that their lives ended, for upon death all mortal souls are his due. However, those condemned that called out for godly intervention but did not include Nagash in their supplications are noted, and grim plans are made for the ultimate fate of those unfortunate souls.

Upon their deaths, the spirit-essence of those that die in captivity but do entreat upon the Lord of Undeath are made into Chainghasts. Infinitely spiteful, the Great Necromancer deems it fitting to keep such souls

eternally imprisoned. Each of these wraith-spirits is encased within an armoured harness further bound with enchanted iron padlocks.

To burden Chainghasts further, Nagash has ordained that each spirit must be tethered to weights bound to heavy chains wrought of black-iron. This cursed metal is alloyed with dreadful emotions – the worst pangs of fear and hopelessness experienced by those callously enslaved. These 'ghastflails' are the weapons with which Chainghasts reap new souls, swinging them in great arcs to bludgeon a bloody path through the foe. When whirled with sufficient force the ghastflails build up a deadly charge of purest misery. Used like a massive sling, a ghastflail can launch this pent-up energy, hurling corrosive bolts of spirit force that eat straight through armour to burn a target's soul.

Chainghasts exist only to serve the Spirit Torment named their master. It is their duty to slay whom he commands, whether in close quarters battle or at range. Thus are the chain-bound spirits sent out to wreak havoc, battering mortal bodies to create a rich harvest of souls to be incarcerated into the arcane jails of the Spirit Torments.

Behind sealed iron masks the Chainghasts' minds retain dim memories of their mortal past. Like some dream half forgotten upon waking, each spirit maintains an inexplicable yearning to be free, an urge to escape from bondage, yet it is a desire upon which they can never act. Chainghasts are bound to automatically obey each and every command of their Spirit Torment. Trapped in a never-ending mind-loop, even their innermost thoughts are but another prison.

WRAITH CAPTAINS

Dotted across a Nighthaunt procession are various spectral sub-commanders and champions. As befits the macabre nature of the ghastly hosts, these individuals are not formal military officers, but rather greater spirits – fell spectres imbued by Nagash with even more formidable powers and malignancy.

GUARDIANS OF SOULS

Each Guardian of Souls is a nexus of undead energy. Once, they were lesser Necromancers that used amethyst magic to further their own cause, yet their arcane knowledge was not enough to keep them alive. Nagash eventually claimed their souls, shaping them to better fit his needs. Now they use their spells not for their own ends, but to summon more Nighthaunts or restore spirits damaged in battle.

In addition to a deadly chill blade or heavy maul of judgement, Guardians of Souls bear either a nightmare lantern or a mortality glass. A nightmare lantern is a ghostly beacon lit by the Flame of Nagashizzar. The mind-chilling smoke they exude does not rise up to the heavens, but instead drifts down towards the field of battle. Nearby Nighthaunts are invigorated by the wafting vapours, and a Guardian of Souls can channel the lantern so that the cold fingers of smoke snake through the earth, beckoning spirits to rise out of their graves or chilling mortal foes to death. A Guardian with a mortality glass can slow time, making oncoming enemies feel as if trapped in a nightmare. The arcane spectre can also use sorcery to distort the hourglass, allowing nearby Nighthaunts to move with terrifying swiftness.

LORD EXECUTIONERS

In the living world executioners are tasked with the ending of life, often by axe stroke or noose. Those that knowingly slay the innocent as well as the guilty – claiming that they are 'just doing their duty' – attract the gaze of Nagash. The same is true for those that enjoy their work too much, even those that seek to repent.

In death – especially those slain by the relatives of the innocents they slaughtered – these headsmen are remade into the spectral form of a Lord Executioner. They are charged by Nagash to slay heroes, champions, kings and anyone that defies his laws.

Lord Executioners each bear a massive decapitating axe, and some carry the phantasmal echoes of accoutrements from their past, such as a gallows, torture wheel or stretching rack. The spectres are also surrounded by skull-faces wreathed in balefire. These visages are the remaining spirits of innocents the executioner slew in life. They harass their killer, haranguing him constantly, but also warding him against dangers, blocking enemy spells and sword blows. They do this not as a kindness, but so he can never escape the executioner's bloodthirsty work.

CAIRN WRAITHS

The souls of only the most sick and twisted mortals descend into the underworlds and become Cairn Wraiths. Most spirits simply devolve, turning into shades that are mere echoes of their former selves, dark fodder for Nagash's fell purposes. Some, however, remain defiant. Those with supreme willpower to endure the spiritual torments that strip away all that they were save their unending hatred. Only the most spiteful of mass murderers endure, and they become Cairn Wraiths – spectres that delight in hacking down mortals to watch their souls seep outwards.

Armed with a reaper scythe, Cairn Wraiths of the past were lone predators that haunted sites where amethyst magic lay heavy, such as battlefields, barrows or areas where some great tragedy occurred. Soulblight vampires sought out these killers and used magic to bind their services, for Cairn Wraiths serve no other willingly. After the floods of death magic unleashed by the Shyish necroquake, the hooded ghasts stalked the Mortal Realms in numbers never before seen. With a single act – the ritualistic building of the Great Cairnoch – Nagash bound them all instantly. Some Cairn Wraiths were shackled into the service of Necromancers, or vampires, but most drifted into Nighthaunt processions, where Knights of Shrouds made quick use of their fearsome combat prowess and eagerness to deal death.

TOMB BANSHEES

Those most betrayed or tormented in life find no succour in death, for they are drawn to an afterlife devoid of rest, filled only with mourning and vengeance. Known as Tomb Banshees, these embittered spirits are fated to shriek their wailing cries and haunt the material plane.

Many wielders of dark magic seek to recruit Tomb Banshees to their cause, for they are deadly opponents. The touch of these ghostly spectres is enough to stop a beating heart, and their chill daggers can pass through armour to deliver a mortal blow. Their most formidable weapon, however, is their scream. The howl of a Tomb Banshee can instantly kill, for it freezes the blood in their victims' veins. The cacophony is so painful it can rip a soul from its physical body. Only the bravest can withstand that aural assault and live.

Tomb Banshees are common within the Nighthaunt processions, where they drift between other spectral formations while delivering their spiteful shrieks to destroy the foe. Although they are most frequently reported as acting alone, there have been whispers following the recent eruption of undead invasions of several Tomb Banshees working in unison. At least five joined together – dubbed the Hellchoir of the Banelands – as part of the army of Baron Finalem. Their screams were instrumental in the successful reclamation of the great burial grounds known as the Vale of Remembrance. There are also tales of a Tomb Banshee leading a vast wave of Myrmourn Banshees, the most famous being the host out of Aqshy known as the Burning Scream.

WRAITH HOSTS

The stench of open graves and mildewed cloth, the unnatural chilling of the air along with the clank of chains and unearthly moans – these announce the presence of the wraith host. Directed by more powerful wills or by their own malicious instincts, wraith hosts of the Nighthaunt processions come to extinguish life wherever they find it.

Misery loves company, and there is no company more dolorous than the ghostly legions of Shyish. They are the lesser spirits of the Nighthaunt processions – the foot soldiers, as it were – although they are unlike the troops of any other army. They do not march, and even the least of the spirits floats or glides. All are ethereal spectres wearing tattered robes that glow from within. Enemy arrows and blades not guided by a stalwart will pass straight through the gheists.

All wraiths – no matter which terrifying form they come in – hate the living. Their spite-filled memories are magnified or twisted in the afterlife by Nagash's malefic curses. Gathered together, they are a howling gale of vengeful spirits that sweeps over the battlefields of the Mortal Realms.

GLAIVEWRAITH STALKERS

Glaivewraith Stalkers prowl in packs, as they did in life. Where once they were mounted hunters that rode down their quarry for the thrill of the chase before the kill, they are now a strange amalgamation of horse and rider. Each of the crook-backed spectres is armed with a wickedly sharp glaive. Once levelled at a target, the Glaivewraith Stalker that bears the weapon never rests until their prey is slain. Always, no many how many twists or turns their journey might require, their blade is drawn directly to the heart of their victim, just as a compass needle is pulled always to its point of reference. The glaive even aims at targets out of sight or over distant horizons, for quarry that has been thus marked has no other destiny but to join the Glaivewraiths in death.

Glaivewraith Stalkers drift steadily after their prey, often advancing to the heartbeat thump of a drum made from human skin. Any thrill of the chase has been long replaced by a cold and unforgiving drive. For the hunted there can be no escape, but the same can be said for the hunter – for a Glaivewraith, there is no satisfaction in slaying their quarry, and a new target is immediately marked for the ritual to begin again.

'The Glaivewraith, it comes for you,
It follows you about.
There's no escape from what it will do,
Old Bones has found you out.'
- Lyrian lullaby

GRIMGHAST REAPERS

In life, those who were to become Grimghast Reapers were careful and meticulous killers. They planned and plotted, worrying over every facet of the illicit deeds that they committed. All took great pains to see that no blood would fall upon their hands, for the deaths were brought about through whispered lies, poison or the employment of mercenaries. In death, Nagash has seen fit to punish such souls with everlasting bloodshed in the most frenzied and obvious manner possible. Blindfolded with strips of sanctified shrouds, Grimghast Reapers cannot see, not even with the witch-sight granted other spirit forms. This is part of their curse to keep them in a state of eternal rage.

Armed with slasher scythes, Grimghast Reapers are indiscriminate killers. They never cease in their long sweeping strokes that mercilessly cut down the enemy a rank at a time, and they never tire. Like horrible clockwork figures, they endlessly repeat their deadly shearing strikes. The grim spectres move quickly, hovering down to attack, but doing so with jarring motions that are antithetical to the graceful movements of the living. They seem to start and stop, travelling in convulsive bursts, yet they are fast for all that.

The champions of the Grimghast Reapers are known as Extollers of Shyish. Once spiritual leaders that spoke out in life against Nagash, they are now harbingers of death. Each bears a massive bell – a death knell – whose sombre toll strikes to honour the Supreme Master of Death. The sound rings especially true when the great bell batters the flesh of the living – the resulting resonance is so disturbing that it can shake a mortal's soul loose from their physical form.

CHAINRASP HORDES

The most numerous of all the spirits that join Nighthaunt processions are the Chainrasp Hordes. These gheists are created from the spirits of the most vicious and irredeemable criminals to have lived in the Mortal Realms.

The form of a Chainrasp echoes the circumstances of their death. They who met their end in chains wear the same bonds in death. Those weighted down with heavy iron cannonballs or trammelled with thick manacles drag that same load with them. Yet no matter what they haul, Chainrasps seek to bludgeon, claw or sink a blade into any living creature they come across. While enemy weapons might pass harmlessly through the chained spectres, their own spiked clubs and rusty swords cleave flesh and break bone as easily as any physical equivalent.

The spectres of the Chainrasp Hordes are lesser spirits, held together in the afterlife only by Nagash's curse and by their own never-ending spite. That hatred leads to a madness so all-consuming that when the darksome beings gather in sufficient number, they leave behind a spiritual frostbite. Over time, this intense negative energy saps their victims' will to fight, making them easy prey when the Chainrasps move to attack.

Chainrasp champions are known as Dreadwardens – the wardens of unrepentant souls. The candles they bear are like beacons to the spirits under their charge, casting a dread light that the Chainrasps believe will lead to their freedom. In fact, it is this eerie glow that helps bind the impenitent to eternal servitude. The Chainrasps may have thought death would be an escape from their terrible imprisonment, but truly, it was only the beginning.

BLADEGHEIST REVENANTS

Moving like a ghostly cyclone, the creatures known as Bladegheist Revenants spin in a frenetic fashion. They are souls taken from those who met particularly tormenting ends – those sealed in spike-ridden encasements, choked beneath water or buried alive. Their last living thoughts were a frenzy of desperation, a last flurry of defiance in an attempt to break free. Thanks to Nagash's terrible curse, that horrible ending moment has been preserved forever in the Bladegheist Revenants.

Still lashing out in a blind frenzy, each Bladegheist Revenant has now been armed with a long sword – a tomb greatblade – that stands nearly as tall as a man. In their maddened fury the revenants spin in arcs, their own momentum pulling them forward in a destructive path that cleaves through the enemy's ranks. Although their other senses are numbed, trapped as they are in a final push for freedom, Bladegheist Revenants can feel the presence of what they imagine to be their captors. Any nearby Spirit Torments or Chainrasp Hordes serve to spur the whirling spectres on to even further manic efforts to escape their imagined doom.

MYRMOURN BANSHEES

The Myrmourn Banshees have a diabolical hunger, for they feast solely upon magic. No enemy spell is safe from the ravenous spirits, and they haunt the Mortal Realms in search of arcane energies to consume.

Myrmourn Banshees are drawn to magic as carrion are drawn to the dead, and such is their bitterness towards life that any mortal creature in their way is likely to receive a swift jab from their cursed chill daggers.

Once, these women were practitioners of magic and seekers of eldritch knowledge, yet in their studies of lore they failed to pay proper respect to the Supreme Lord of the Undead. Upon their demise, Nagash decided that since in life they desired magic so much, they should continue that way in the afterlife.

Wrapped in tattered robes and funeral shrouds, Myrmourn Banshees have lost the ability to use their physical senses, and can now only detect the magic that they crave and the living creatures that they jealously detest. An opposing wizard has little chance of successfully casting spells near a large enough pack of Myrmourn Banshees, for they will simply devour incantations before they can have any effect. The sudden infusion of arcane energies causes the lithe spectres to gleam with fell power – especially their chill daggers – though it does nothing to sate their greed for more magic.

DREADSCYTHE HARRIDANS

Dreadscythe Harridans were once healers and nurturing types, women devoted to easing suffering and prolonging life. It is, doubtlessly, these very offenses that drew the attention of Nagash. To deny the Great Necromancer his souls at their rightfully appointed time is to earn a cold ire that is unlike any other.

Nagash waits for no mortal, nor does he tolerate any interfering with his plans. It was imperative that he teach any such miscreants and interlopers a lesson. Truly, none would forestall death. So did Nagash prepare a special reward in the afterlife for those guilty of such crimes – the dreadful Harridan Curse. This baleful hex twisted the offending souls, reshaping them into something that was quite the opposite of what they once were.

Where there were once healing hands now grow bonescythes – horrible reaping instruments intended for murder. If their demeanour had been gentle and caring, the Dreadscythe Harridans – as they came to be called – are now raging killers. In life the sight of blood and injuries stirred in them compassion, but now it only incites greater fury. And lips that uttered gentle and soothing words to ease a patient's qualms now issue incomprehensible bloodthirsty shrieks that cause all but the bravest to quake with fear. Unable to enunciate, the Harridans only grow angrier. Those who led in life do so also in death – at the fore of Dreadscythe Harridan packs are the Slasher Crones, the most formidable killers of all their kind.

Perhaps the most disturbing consequence of the Harridan Curse is that the minds of the former healers are intact and aware. Most spectres lose all aspects of their mortal lives, but not so the Dreadscythe Harridans. While they retain their old memories they can no longer control their actions, so each is cognisant of and bears full witness to the atrocities that they commit, yet can do nothing to halt.

'The grave is wide, the grave is deep,
Pray do not come for me in my sleep.
Every Lyrian must always learn,
Those that go, sometimes return.
Born of night, they hunt the dark,
With unseeing eyes, dead and stark.
The grave is wide, the grave is deep,
Blessed forever to always sleep.'
- Lyrian children's rhyme
for the dead

SPECTRAL SHOCK FORCES

Weaving in between the larger formations of the Nighthaunt processions are smaller shock forces. As the wraith hordes surround the foe these hard-hitting spectres strike, unleashing their hatred upon the living. For many enemies, the last sight they witness are Spirit Hosts, Hexwraiths or a Black Coach bearing down upon them.

SPIRIT HOSTS

Some of the most commonly encountered wraiths across the Mortal Realms are the Spirit Hosts. Even before the Shyish necroquake Spirit Hosts were known to stalk ancient cairns, battlefields or sites of horrific trauma. They rise out of the ground, mist-like, for they are the spirits of the damned, stripped of body and individuality and fused into a roiling mass of ethereal energy. Amidst the swirls are deathly faces and grasping talons that snatch out to grab and torment the living.

Spirit Hosts are amongst the lowest of spectral forms. They are clusters of souls merged into one spirit cloud, and like the bodies piled into a mass grave, they are devoid of any identity. All memory and form has dissolved

save for a cold hatred of the living, for in mortal-kind they recognise a flicker of that which they have lost.

Spirit Hosts are deadly foes – their phantom weapons and raking claws rend not only flesh, but the soul as well. Their chill touch can pass through armour and bone to grasp organs or stab deep into vitals. When the processions muster for war Spirit Hosts flock to join them.

HEXWRAITHS

Also known as Reaper Knights, Hexwraiths are fell riders astride ghostly steeds. They charge forward illuminated by strange balefires, swinging their eerily glowing scythes in deadly arcs. A single swipe from such a weapon can cut the cord

between a soul and its body, allowing it to be claimed by the wielder. The flickering flames that surround Hexwraiths are the smouldering remnants of the spirit-stuff these dread cavalrymen have stolen during their rampages.

In the past, Hexwraiths rose to haunt battlefields, riding down mortals in order to claim their souls. The spectral riders were often recruited as shock elements into Nagash's undead legions, but since the Shyish necroquake it is in the Nighthaunt processions where the Hexwraiths are most often encountered. Striking hard and fast, they gallop over rivers and through walls to pursue the enemy, their cruel laughter echoing across the battlefield as their terrified foes attempt to flee in vain.

THE BLACK COACH

The mightiest blow or spell can unbind the spirits of the undead, destroying them. However, the most powerful of these creatures – most notably Soulblight vampires, lichelords or the most adept of Necromancers – can survive the destruction of their material form. Driven by a dark will, their malevolent animus begins to gather and re-form a new physical shell.

The Black Coaches are funerary carriages from the underworlds. Within these arcane vehicles any tangible remains – be they ashes, bones, or leathery scraps of skin – are gathered in a casket that offers a safe haven in which the banished entity can reform. The dormant occupant can feed upon the energies of death, drinking in agony and grief in order to grow stronger.

Pulled by four skeletal Nightmare steeds, the Black Coach speeds forward at a considerable pace. The driver is a Cairn Wraith who either wields a two-handed reaper scythe or employs the nightmarish soulreach grasp, their spectral hands ranging out impossibly far to pluck out a victim's very soul. Hovering about the unholy carriage are wraith-like relic bearers, each carrying an artefact important to the recovering being. The Black Coach is phantasmal in nature, unbound by the physical world. Its wheels run over pits and precipices, leaving the ground altogether in order to clear obstacles, although it may also choose to simply pass through them.

Black Coaches are drawn towards battlefields, for there the power of death is strongest. From atop the coach the Cairn Wraith targets nearby enemies while the iron-bound wheels and pounding hooves of the steeds crush foes beneath them. Gliding from the skies above, the relic bearers dart in to deliver blows with their spectral talons. All of this violence only helps to fuel the death magic that is absorbed by the malefic thing in the coffin. By drawing off those dark energies, the being within the casket grows stronger, its aura of malice expanding ever outwards. As this happens, the Black Coach becomes an even deadlier threat to its foes.

On first tasting death, the Black Coach speeds forward before shimmering jets of balefire extend from the wheels, acting like scythes to cut down enemies. When the coach is immersed in sufficient energies it flickers, allowing it to disappear only to reappear in a more advantageous position. As the hellish vehicle continues to absorb power, the souls of the freshly slain are subsumed, healing the coach and exuding a nimbus of fell light. With enough death magic nearby, the witchfires of the Black Coach blaze outwards, scorching any who draw near. So does the Black Coach hurtle across the battlefield, reaping the foe and feeding its dark passenger. Onwards it rolls, growing ever more powerful until it becomes a nigh-unstoppable force of death.

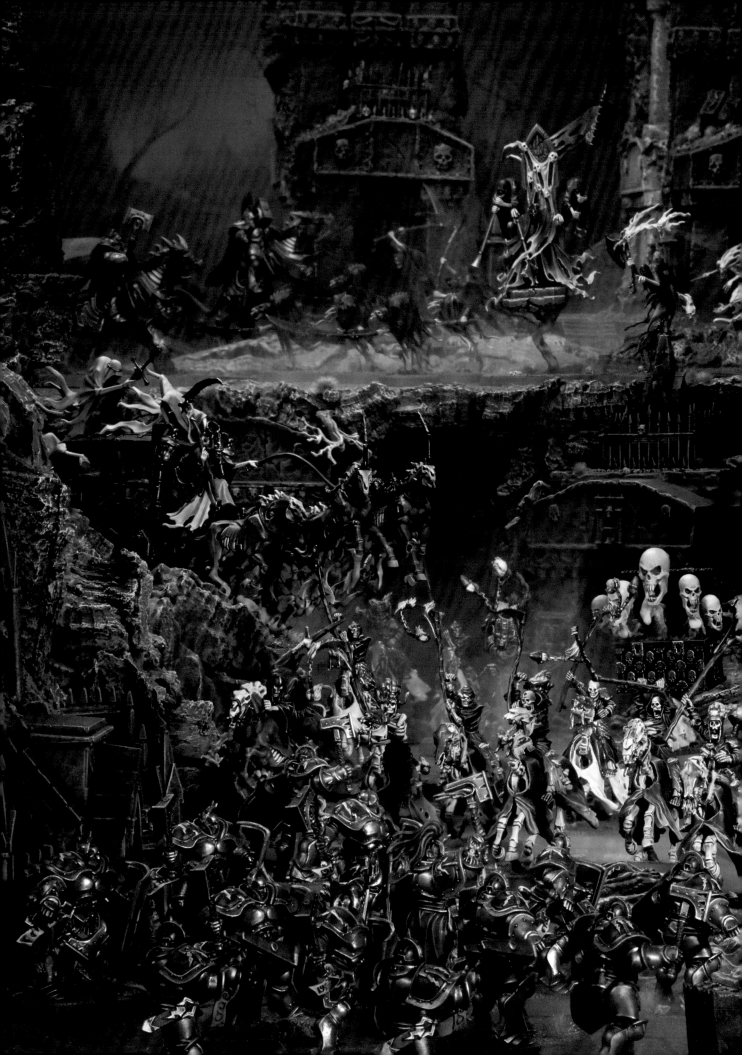

From cairns and crypts untold, Lady Olynder, Mortarch of Grief, summons forth the Nighthaunt processions. Their attacks will spread shock and terror across the Mortal Realms.

THE SPECTRAL HOSTS

With their flowing ethereal robes, dynamic poses and myriad macabre details heavy with deathly symbolism, Nighthaunt Citadel Miniatures are darkly inspiring to behold. Here we present a showcase of Nighthaunt models expertly painted by Games Workshop's very own 'Eavy Metal Team and Design Studio army painters.

Beneath a pall of crippling sorrow, Lady Olynder leads a Nighthaunt procession into battle against Sigmar's Stormcast Eternals. With Kurdoss Valentian at her side, there will be no mercy shown towards anything that lives.

Lady Olynder, Mortarch of Grief

Kurdoss Valentian, the Craven King

Knight of Shrouds

Knight of Shrouds on Ethereal Steed

Where the dreaded wraith-wizard Reikenor the Grimhailer appears, there death is sure to follow. Sweeping down from the skies upon his winged steed, Kyllaron, Reikenor reaps souls by the command of Nagash and Lady Olynder.

With a wave of terror spreading before them, a Knight of Shrouds and a Shroudguard – a protective circle of frenzied Bladegheist Revenants – lead a Nighthaunt procession in a shock assault.

Bladegheist Revenants

Lord Executioner

A Dreadblade Harrow materialises suddenly on the battlefield, galloping ahead of the Hexwraiths to spread terror amongst the enemy. With its ability to discorporate, the foe begins to fear where this spectral rider will appear next.

Led by a Lord Executioner, the Spirit Hosts of an Execution Horde scream out of the mists in a sudden attack that tears through a group of Blood Warriors like a spectral tempest.

Sweeping out of the underworlds, Deathriders – a Black Coach, Dreadblade Harrow and Hexwraiths – charge headlong into Nurgle's daemons, cleaving through them entirely.

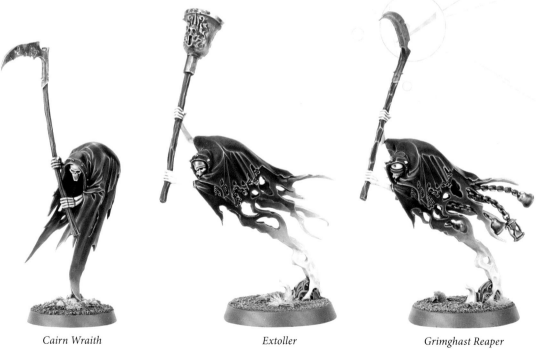

Cairn Wraith   *Extoller*   *Grimghast Reaper*

When the balefires burn pale and the dread moon rises, the Nighthaunts stalk the rising mists, claiming souls in the name of Nagash. Victims can run, but from a foe that can pass through walls, they cannot hide.

Glaivewraith Stalker   Deathbeat Drummer   Myrmourn Banshee   Tomb Banshee

Chainghast

Spirit Torment

Chainghast

Guardian of Souls

Slasher Crone

Dreadscythe Harridan

Dreadwarden

Chainrasp Hordes

Cursed to forever haunt the living, the spectral hosts sweep over the battlefield like some phantasmal fog. To see such horrors is to see your own doom.

PAINTING YOUR NIGHTHAUNTS

Whether you have never painted a Citadel Miniature in your life or are a master of the brush with decades of experience, the prospect of painting a Nighthaunt procession offers a unique and exciting challenge. Following are some tips and examples to get you started with painting your own spectral horde.

There is nothing like the sight of a fully painted army of Citadel Miniatures. There is real satisfaction to be had in adding your chosen colours, teasing out the finely sculpted details, and truly making your miniatures collection your own. After all, one painted spectre looks great, but an entire phantasmal army brought together through shared colours is something even more fantastic. For those of us that are completionists, there is also immense gratification in watching your collection grow as you add each new painted figure to the ranks of the finished models.

There's no right or wrong way to go about painting your collection of miniatures. Some people revel in treating each miniature as a work of art, lavishing attention on every inch of every model and painstakingly crafting scenic bases. Others prefer a far simpler approach with basic

paint jobs that allow them to quickly assemble legions of finished models. And, of course, there is plenty of middle ground for those that enjoy painting their troops but devote even more attention to key figures such as heroes, war machines and monsters. Again, there is no one way to paint, just the way that works best for you.

The spirit-ridden army of the Nighthaunts has its own ghastly aesthetic – tormented apparitions that have risen straight out of the underworlds. Your first decision will be to choose a paint scheme for your miniatures. The colours you select are very likely to influence the character of your army – are they pale and cold, glowing eerily, or faded almost to nothing? Examples of the different colours Nighthaunts can exhibit are shown on the following pages and in the images throughout this book, but of course it is also possible to create your own.

Painting Citadel Miniatures is vastly rewarding. The more you put in, the more you get out. Before painting your models, however, you'll first need to assemble them. To begin with, you'll want to follow the advice given in the construction booklet, but as your confidence grows you may find yourself customising your miniatures by combining different weapons and modifying their poses.

The Citadel Paint System takes the guesswork out of painting, and uses several different formulations of paint to best match different techniques. The paints are used in a set sequence, and each enhances the underlying colour to produce a final scheme that belies the straightforward techniques.

The first paint you'll apply is called the undercoat. Supplied in spray cans, it's formulated to provide a smooth, even surface for the colours that follow. Once it has dried, you can break out your brushes and start bringing your miniature to (un)life. The following stage-by-stage guides present the colours and techniques we used to paint the Nighthaunts, but there are no 'rules' as to the colours you use for your own models – the Mortal Realms are a limitless canvas, so it's entirely up to you.

Base paints contain a high percentage of pigment, and deliver bold, intense colour that provides the foundation for the paint scheme. Neat basecoats are key to a great-looking miniature, and two thin coats are almost always better than one thick coat.

Shade paints are almost the consistency of ink, and are designed to run into the model's recesses to create depth and contrast. They are usually applied all over an area as a wash, or painted directly into recesses such as the gaps between armour plates.

Dry paints are applied using a technique called drybrushing, which involves passing a very lightly loaded brush rapidly across the model to apply a dusting of colour to the raised detail. It's a very quick way of adding highlights to a miniature.

Layer paints are brighter colours than Base paints, and have a smoother consistency. They are usually applied all over an underlying Base colour to achieve a more vibrant hue, or are painted in focused lines along raised areas and edges as highlights.

WARHAMMER TV

Warhammer TV's painting tutorials have insights for everyone, as they show you how to paint Citadel Miniatures from start to finish. The guides are available for free on games-workshop.com, and can also be watched via the Warhammer TV YouTube channel. Why not take a moment to check them out?

GHASTLY DETAILS

There are a variety of techniques you can use when painting Nighthaunts, a wide selection of which are shown on the following pages. Many of these techniques can be applied no matter which Nighthaunt model you are working on. The tips contained in this painting guide will prove useful even if you have devised your own colour scheme.

BLUE SPIRIT - LAYERING TECHNIQUE

   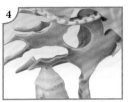

1 Apply a basecoat of Ionrach Skin over a Corax White Spray undercoat.

2 Apply a thin wash of the Technical paint Nighthaunt Gloom.

3 Re-apply a layer of Ionrach Skin, being careful to avoid the deeper grooves and recesses.

4 Finish off with a fine edge highlight using Deepkin Flesh.

GREEN SPIRIT - DRYBRUSHING TECHNIQUE

 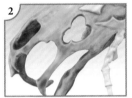  

Begin with an undercoat of Corax White Spray.

Apply a thin wash of the Technical paint Hexwraith Flame.

Finish off by lightly drybrushing with Longbeard Grey.

Alternate: Ulthuan Grey base, Waywatcher Green glaze, Ulthuan Grey layer, White Scar highlight

CLOTH

1 Apply a basecoat of Incubi Darkness.

2 Use a wash of Nuln Oil to darken and add depth to the creases and folds.

3 Apply a highlight of Kabalite Green to the raised areas and edges.

4 Finish off with a fine edge highlight of Dawnstone.

CLOTH VARIANTS

Rhinox Hide, Nuln Oil wash, Gorthor Brown layer, Karak Stone edge highlight

Skavenblight Dinge, Agrax Earthshade wash, Dawnstone highlight

Abaddon Black, Stegadon Scale Green and Russ Grey edge highlights

Screamer Pink, Nuln Oil wash, Pink Horror and Cadian Fleshtone edge highlights

RUSTED METAL

1

A basecoat of Leadbelcher is applied over a Chaos Black undercoat.

2

The second step is to give the metal a heavy wash of Agrax Earthshade.

3

Using a combination of drybrushing and stippling, add Ryza Rust in patches across the metal.

4

The final stage is Stormhost Silver used as an edge highlight and to paint small scratches.

VERDIGRIS BRASS

1

A basecoat of Fulgurite Copper is applied over a Chaos Black undercoat.

2

Apply a wash of Agrax Earthshade, working it into all the bell's nooks and details.

3

A thin edge highlight of Stormhost Silver picks out the high points.

4

The final stage is to stipple Nihilakh Oxide into a few recesses.

WEAPON VARIANTS

Incubi Darkness, Nuln Oil wash, Kabalite Green and Dawnstone edge highlights

Leadbelcher basecoat, Nuln Oil wash, Stormhost Silver highlight, Blood For The Blood God stipple

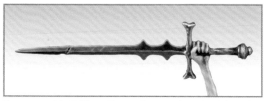

Basecoat with Caliban Green, then wash with Nuln Oil. Next, layer with Warpstone Glow, then Moot Green. Finish with edge highlights of Flash Gitz Yellow.

BALEFIRE

1

Apply a coat of Ulthuan Grey over the top of a Corax White undercoat.

2

A wash of Biel-Tan Green is generously applied to the flames.

3

The next step is to apply a glaze of Lamenters Yellow.

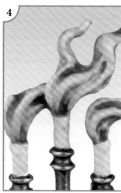

4

A final edge highlight of Pallid Wych Flesh picks out the swirling flame tips.

CANDLES

1 Apply a basecoat of Screamer Pink over a Corax White undercoat.

2 Wash the candles all over with Nuln Oil.

3 Highlight the upper portions of the candles with Pink Horror.

4 Pick out the dripping wax using fine highlights of Cadian Fleshtone.

LANTERN GLOW

1 Basecoat the glass with Ulthuan Grey.

2 Apply a wash of Hexwraith Flame to the glass areas.

3 A Layer of 'Ardcoat gives the glass a shiny, reflective appearance.

Tip: For a cooler lantern glow effect, substitute Hexwraith Flame for Nighthaunt Gloom.

Lantern Housing: Fulgurite Copper, Agrax Earthshade wash, Sycorax Bronze layer, Stormhost Silver highlight, Sotek Green in the recesses

OTHER DETAILS

Steed: Incubi Darkness basecoat, Nuln Oil wash, Thunderhawk Blue layer, Karak Stone highlight

Wood: Abaddon Black basecoat, Eshin Grey drybrush, Administratum Grey drybrush

Grave: Mechanicus Standard Grey basecoat, Agrax Earthshade wash, Dawnstone drybrush

Hourglass: Warpfiend Grey basecoat, Xereus Purple layer, Fenrisian Grey highlight, 'Ardcoat

Bone 1: Rhinox Hide basecoat, Gorthor Brown layer, Karak Stone layer, Ushabti Bone highlight

Bone 2: Screaming Skull, Coelia Greenshade and Lahmian Medium (1:1), White Scar highlight

Blending: Thin your paint with Lahmian Medium and build up the effect using several thin coats.

Hair: Ushabti Bone, Biel-Tan Green wash, Nuln Oil Gloss wash, Screaming Skull drybrush

SHOCK AND TERROR

On Nagash's command, Lady Olynder has organised the Nighthaunts into processions and sent them into the Mortal Realms as the speartip of the Great Necromancer's Soul Wars. There are many ways to collect a Nighthaunt army, and this spread offers one example of how a procession can be assembled.

When collecting a Warhammer Age of Sigmar army, it's a good idea to have a plan. How you decide which units to include in your Nighthaunt procession might be based on the look of the models, how you envision them performing during a tabletop battle, or could follow a narrative found in a battletome or even one of your own invention. There is no single right way to collect your army, only the way you deem best. The goal is the same – to field a battle-ready Nighthaunt procession! Here is how we assembled the collection shown below.

The first model we chose for our procession was none other than Lady Olynder. On the tabletop her aura-based abilities make her an ideal commander, boosting friendly troops around her and punishing those of the enemy. Our main reason for including her, however, was the sheer characterfulness of the model – her veiled visage and banshee handmaidens are the perfect level of ghastly creepiness for our army's leader.

A Knight of Shrouds gives the army another strong hero – his command

ability raises the combat potential of nearby Nighthaunt units, so we imagine sending him charging into the thick of the fighting.

The largest unit in this collection is that of the Chainrasp Hordes. These long-suffering spirits will be used to bog the enemy down. Their own losses can be replaced by the Guardian of Souls, who is able to use his nightmare lantern to make the troops more effective, and his Spectral Lure spell to raise more spirits, ensuring the foe stays locked in grinding combat. The Nighthaunts

possess a slew of small units effective at manoeuvring around close combats in order to launch their own devastating assaults into enemy flanks. Spirit Hosts are ideal for this, and are even better when led by a Lord Executioner, as this completes the Execution Horde warscroll battalion and unlocks a rules bonus. The Spirit Torment and Chainghasts are another combination that works well alongside the Chainrasp Horde. While getting into position, the Spirit Torment augments nearby friendly units, and heals them as well. The Chainghasts meanwhile excel on the front line, as the more foes that are around them, the more damage they will cause.

Other particularly hard-hitting Nighthaunt units include Dreadscythe Harridans and Bladegheist Revenants, both of whom unleash an impressive number of armour-piercing attacks. A Tomb Banshee – being a single model – can easily work around the scrum of close combat, slaying enemies with her shrieking howl. Pivotal to this army's offensive power is the Black Coach, which gains new abilities each battle round, growing more deadly as the game progresses. It also serves as another fantastic centrepiece model. Myrmourn Banshees can aid the attack, but are especially useful for destroying enemy spells.

As a whole, this Nighthaunt procession presents a collector and painter with a great variety of phantasmal troops, as well as a competitive tabletop force with many exciting gaming options.

1. Lady Olynder, Mortarch of Grief
2. Knight of Shrouds on Ethereal Steed
3. Tomb Banshee
4. Dreadscythe Harridans
5. Hexwraiths
6. Black Coach
7. Lord Executioner
8. Spirit Hosts
9. Spirit Torment
10. Chainghasts
11. Guardian of Souls
12. Glaivewraith Stalkers
13. Cairn Wraith
14. Grimghast Reapers
15. Chainrasp Horde
16. Bladegheist Revenants
17. Myrmourn Banshees

'Do not cease the attack until every living soul has been sent to join us in the underworlds!'

- Lady Olynder

THE NIGHTHAUNT PROCESSIONS

This battletome contains all of the rules you need to field your Nighthaunt miniatures on the battlefields of the Mortal Realms, from a host of exciting allegiance abilities to a range of warscrolls and warscroll battalions. The rules are split into the following sections.

ALLEGIANCE ABILITIES
This section describes the allegiance abilities available to a Nighthaunt army. The rules for how to use the following allegiance abilities can be found in the core rules.

BATTLE TRAITS
Abilities available to every unit in a Nighthaunt army (pg 53).

COMMAND TRAITS
Abilities available to the general of a Nighthaunt army if it is a **Hero** (pg 54).

SPELL LORES
Spells available to **Wizards** in a Nighthaunt army (pg 55).

ARTEFACTS OF POWER
Artefacts available to **Heroes** in a Nighthaunt army (pg 56-57).

BATTLEPLANS
This section includes a new narrative battleplan that can be played with a Nighthaunt army.

Battleplan: Death From Within enables you to surprise your foes within their own stronghold, as your Nighthaunt host bursts forth from the underworlds to assail them.

PATH TO GLORY
This section contains rules for using your Nighthaunt collection in Path to Glory campaigns (pg 60-63).

WARSCROLLS
This section includes all of the warscrolls you will need to play games of Warhammer Age of Sigmar with your Nighthaunt miniatures.

There are three types of warscroll included in this section:

WARSCROLL BATTALIONS
These are formations made up of several Nighthaunt units that combine their strengths to gain powerful new abilities (pg 64-71).

WARSCROLLS
A warscroll for each unit is included here. The rules for using a Nighthaunt unit, along with its characteristics and abilities, are detailed on its warscroll (pg 72-85).

ENDLESS SPELL WARSCROLLS
There are three endless spell warscrolls that introduce the rules for unique and powerful spells that can be summoned by **Nagash, Supreme Lord of the Undead,** and **Nighthaunt Wizards** (pg 86-87).

PITCHED BATTLE PROFILES
This section contains Pitched Battle profiles for the units, warscroll battalions and endless spells in this book (pg 88).

ALLIES
This section also contains a list of the allies a Nighthaunt army can include.

ALLEGIANCE ABILITIES
BATTLE TRAITS

ASPECTS OF THE ETHEREAL HOSTS

AURA OF DREAD
The very existence of the Nighthaunts is a stark reminder of the terrible fate that awaits those that have displeased Nagash upon death. To face them in battle is to witness these darkest fears made manifest, and can chill the soul of even the most stoic warrior.

Subtract 1 from the Bravery characteristic of enemy units while they are within 6" of any friendly NIGHTHAUNT units.

DEATHLESS SPIRITS
The spirit forms of Nighthaunt warriors are made more formidable by the presence of their lords and masters.

Roll a dice each time you allocate a wound or mortal wound to a friendly NIGHTHAUNT model from a unit wholly within 12" of your general or a friendly NIGHTHAUNT HERO. On a 6+, that wound or mortal wound is negated.

FROM THE UNDERWORLDS THEY COME
None is safe from Nagash's vengeance, for the Nighthaunts can be summoned forth from the underworlds by their spectral overseers, appearing as if from nowhere to assail their prey.

Instead of setting up a NIGHTHAUNT unit on the battlefield, you can place it to one side and say that it is set up in the underworlds as a reserve unit. You can set up one unit in the underworlds for each unit you set up on the battlefield. At the end of your movement phase you can set up any of these units more than 9" from any enemy models. This counts as their move for that turn. Any units which are not set up on the battlefield before the start of the fourth battle round are slain.

FEED ON TERROR
The lords of the Nighthaunts are strengthened by the fear they sow, and can drink deep of this uncontrolled emotion and siphon fresh strength.

Each time an enemy unit fails a battleshock test, pick one friendly NIGHTHAUNT HERO within 6" of that enemy unit. Heal 1 wound that has been allocated to that HERO.

WAVE OF TERROR
On many occasions, entire battlelines have been overrun by a swarming Nighthaunt host without even raising a blade in their own defence.

If you make an unmodified charge roll of 10+ for a friendly NIGHTHAUNT unit, it can fight immediately after you complete the charge move. This does not stop the unit from being picked to fight in the combat phase of the same turn.

COMMAND ABILITY
Spectral Summons: *A Nighthaunt commander can call his ghostly minions to his side in an instant, wherever they may be.*

You can use this command ability at the start of your movement phase. If you do so, pick a friendly NIGHTHAUNT unit that is on the battlefield. Remove that unit from the battlefield, and then set it up wholly within 12" of your general and more than 9" from any enemy models. This counts as their move for that movement phase.

RETURNING SLAIN MODELS
Several Nighthaunt abilities allow you to return slain models to a unit. When you do so, set up the models one at a time within 1" of a model from the unit they are returning to (this can be a model you returned to the unit earlier in the same phase).

The slain models you return to a unit can only be set up within 3" of an enemy unit if one or more models from the unit they are returning to are already within 3" of an enemy unit.

COMMAND TRAITS

SHADES OF DEATH

D6 Command Trait

1 Hatred of the Living: *It is easy to stoke the deep loathing the spirits of the Nighthaunts feel for those who still live.*

You can re-roll failed hit rolls for attacks made with this general's melee weapons unless the target has the **DEATH** keyword.

2 Terrifying Entity: *Some powerful spirits take a gruesome appearance or an overwhelming aura of horror to entire new heights.*

At the start of the enemy movement phase, roll a dice for each enemy unit within 3" of this model. If the roll is equal to or greater than that enemy unit's Bravery characteristic, that unit must make a retreat move in that movement phase.

3 Lingering Spirit: *So much amethyst magic exists within this spirit that its ethereal form is more resilient than most.*

Add 1 to this general's Wounds characteristic.

4 Spiteful Spirit: *This gheist's bitter resentment of its cruel existence is palpable, and can be channelled into a vengeful curse to punish those who would do it harm.*

Roll a dice each time you allocate a wound to this general that was inflicted by a melee weapon. On a 5+, the attacking unit suffers 1 mortal wound after all of its attacks have been made.

5 Cloaked in Shadow: *Eerily intangible, this spirit's ethereal form fades in and out of existence like some wispy cloud of supernatural mist.*

Subtract 1 from hit rolls for attacks made with missile weapons that target this general.

6 Ruler of the Spirit Hosts: *The dark will and deathly power of this spirit are like a siren call, an unseen signal that beckons to others from beyond the grave.*

At the start of your hero phase, you can pick a friendly **SUMMONABLE NIGHTHAUNT** unit within 9" of this general and return D3 slain models to that unit. The returning models must be set up within 9" of this general.

SPELL LORES

You can choose or roll for one of the following spells for each **WIZARD** in a Nighthaunt army.

LORE OF THE UNDERWORLDS

D6 **Spell**

1 **Soul Cage:** *This supernatural cage of phantasmal energies pins opponents in place so that the reaping might begin.*

Soul Cage has a casting value of 6. If successfully cast, pick an enemy unit within 12" of the caster that is visible to them. Until the start of your next hero phase, that unit cannot retreat. In addition, until the start of your next hero phase, that unit cannot fight in the combat phase unless all other enemy units that are eligible to fight have already done so.

2 **Spirit Drain:** *With but a series of fell words of power the caster can whittle away a mortal's life-force, causing their very spirit to seep out of their physical form.*

Spirit Drain has a casting value of 4. If successfully cast, pick an enemy model within 18" of the caster that is visible to them. Roll a number of dice equal to that model's Wounds characteristic. For each 6+, that model's unit suffers 1 mortal wound.

3 **Lifestealer:** *Life hangs upon but a slender thread; this incantation can sever that cord, causing healthy foes to drop like puppets shorn of their strings. Each such death increases the caster's own vitality.*

Lifestealer has a casting value of 7. If successfully cast, pick an enemy unit within 12" of the caster that is visible to them. That unit suffers D3 mortal wounds. For each mortal wound suffered by the enemy unit, you can heal 1 wound allocated to the caster.

4 **Reaping Scythe:** *The caster's weapon extends into a phantasmal scythe, gleaming with fell purpose and honed to razor sharpness.*

Reaping Scythe has a casting value of 4. If successfully cast, pick one of the caster's weapons. Until the start of your next hero phase, you can re-roll failed hit and wound rolls for attacks made with that weapon.

5 **Shademist:** *A supernatural mist envelops the targeted unit, causing them to glimmer as they fade in and out of reality, becoming more baleful and intangible.*

Shademist has a casting value of 6. If successfully cast, pick a friendly **NIGHTHAUNT** unit wholly within 12" of the caster that is visible to them. Subtract 1 from wound rolls for attacks that target that unit until the start of your next hero phase.

6 **Spectral Tether:** *The correct sorcerous incantations can create a temporary link between a powerful Nighthaunt and the underworlds, where it can be restored by drawing upon the amethyst energies of Shyish.*

Spectral Tether has a casting value of 6. If successfully cast, pick a friendly **NIGHTHAUNT HERO** within 12" of the caster. Heal D3 wounds that have been allocated to that unit.

ARTEFACTS OF POWER

WEAPONS OF THE DAMNED

D6 Artefact of Power

1 Shadow's Edge: *It is impossible to tell if this ebon blade is corporeal or mere shadow, yet its touch tears through flesh and bone with ease.*

Pick one of the bearer's melee weapons. If the unmodified hit roll for an attack made with that weapon is 6, that attack inflicts D3 mortal wounds and the attack sequence ends (do not make a wound or save roll).

2 Reaper of Sorrows: *This phantasmal blade harvests emotions, hewing life-force but leaving its victims unmarked save for a horrified rictus.*

Pick one of the bearer's melee weapons. Before attacking with that weapon, roll 2D6. If the roll is higher than the target unit's Bravery, that weapon's Rend characteristic is -3 for attacks made against that unit.

3 Balefire Blade: *This blade is alight with the burning souls of sacrificed prophets and seers who dared to challenge the wielder's authority.*

Pick one of the bearer's melee weapons. Add 1 to that weapon's Damage characteristic.

4 Slitter: *Forged from the shivs and cut-throat razors of a thousand serial killers, this dagger is murder made manifest.*

After picking the bearer to fight, before they pile in you can pick one enemy model within 1" of the bearer and roll a dice; if the roll is greater than that model's Wounds characteristic, it is slain.

5 Headsman's Judgement: *This weapon has gained in power for the innumerable condemned souls it has sent screaming into the afterlife.*

Pick one of the bearer's melee weapons. Add 1 to hit and wound rolls for attacks made with that weapon.

6 Shrieking Blade: *This blade emits an unnerving, mournful howl that only exacerbates the horrifying nature of its wielder.*

Subtract 1 from hit rolls for attacks made with melee weapons that target the bearer.

RELICS OF THE UNDERWORLDS

D6   **Artefact of Power**

1   **Cloak of the Waxing Moon:** *Each blade that passes through the wispy folds of this dark garment begins to lose its substance as it too becomes ethereal.*

The Deathless Spirits battle trait negates wounds inflicted by melee weapons that are allocated to the bearer on a 5+ instead of 6+.

2   **Pendant of the Fell Wind:** *A chill gale blows ever behind the wearer of this dark trinket, carrying them into battle on gusts of suffocating air.*

You can add 3" to normal moves made by friendly **NIGHTHAUNT** units that are wholly within 12" of the bearer at the start of that normal move.

3   **Dreadbolt Ring:** *Gouts of lashing green flames leap forth from this ring as it devours the souls of those slain by the wearer.*

When the bearer fights, if they inflict one or more wounds with their melee weapons, you can inflict D3 mortal wounds on one enemy unit within 3" of the bearer after all of the bearer's attacks have been made.

4   **Mirror of Screaming Souls:** *A mirror of polished shadeglass, this looking-glass houses the wailing souls of those that stared too long at their own reflection.*

At the start of your shooting phase, roll 2D6 for each enemy unit within 8" of the bearer. If the roll is higher than that unit's Bravery characteristic, it suffers 1 mortal wound.

5   **Midnight Tome:** *Only the lifeless can read the spells and incantations inscribed upon the pitch-black pages of this cursed grimoire.*

The bearer becomes a **WIZARD** and knows the Arcane Bolt and Mystic Shield spells, as well as one spell from the Lore of the Underworlds (pg 55). They can attempt to cast one spell in each of your hero phases, and attempt to unbind one spell in each enemy hero phase. If the bearer was already a **WIZARD**, they can attempt to cast 1 additional spell in each of your hero phases instead.

6   **Covetous Familiar:** *This spiteful poltergeist swirls around its master's essence, lashing out at any other soul that draws too close.*

At the start of the combat phase, roll a dice for each enemy unit within 3" of the bearer. On a 2+, that unit suffers 1 mortal wound.

INFERNAL LANTERNS

GUARDIAN OF SOULS with Nightmare Lantern only.

D3   **Artefact of Power**

1   **Lightshard of the Harvest Moon:** *Once released, the baleful light of this lantern fills the battlefield with an eerie glow, readying the enemy for the reaping.*

Once per battle, at the start of the combat phase, the bearer can use this artefact. If they do so, you can re-roll failed hit rolls for attacks made by friendly **NIGHTHAUNT** units that are wholly within 12" of the bearer when they attack in that combat phase.

2   **Wychlight Lantern:** *The otherworldly incense that billows from this lantern merges with the bearer's spectral form, lending them great power.*

Add 1 to casting rolls for the bearer.

3   **Beacon of Nagashizzar:** *The malignant light of Nagashizzar burns within this fell lantern with even greater intensity.*

If the bearer successfully casts the Spectral Lure spell and it is not unbound, instead of the normal effects of the spell, you can either heal D6+3 wounds that have been allocated to the target unit or, if no wounds have been allocated to that unit, you can return a number of slain models to it that have a combined Wounds characteristic equal to or less than D6+3.

BATTLEPLAN
DEATH FROM WITHIN

The mightiest fortresses of the Mortal Realms are nigh unassailable, their towering walls and imposing defences all but impervious to assault by land or air. Yet to Nagash's Nighthaunt hosts, able to tear through the veil of reality from the underworlds wherever their immortal master commands, such defences are rendered entirely obsolete.

The battle is being fought in a courtyard behind the stronghold's main walls – an area thought safe from assault so long as the walls could be held…

THE ARMIES
Each player picks an army as described in the core rules. One player is the Nighthaunt player and their opponent is the Defender. The Nighthaunt player must use a Nighthaunt army.

THE BATTLEFIELD
The Defender sets up any terrain as they see fit, though they must set up at least one terrain feature wholly within each of their territories.

SIEGE TARGETS
After setting the battlefield, the Defender picks one terrain feature in each of their territories to be the Nighthaunt player's siege targets (see Glorious Victory).

SET-UP
The Defender sets up their army first. Defending units must be set up wholly within one of the Defender's two territories.

The Nighthaunt player then alternates setting up one unit wholly within their territory, and one unit in the underworlds (see From The Underworlds They Come on page 53), repeating these steps until they have set up all of their units.

FIRST TURN
The Nighthaunt player has the first turn in the first battle round.

TAKEN OFF GUARD
The defender's forces have reacted with admirable haste to the sudden danger within their midst, but are still reeling from the unexpected quarter from which they are now assailed, throwing their command structure into disarray.

The Defender cannot spend any command points in the first battle round.

UNDERWORLD ATTACK
A fresh wave of Nighthaunts lies in wait to pour forth from the underworlds and sweep into the stronghold's hapless defenders.

Add 1 to charge rolls for **NIGHTHAUNT** units that arrived from reserve in the same turn.

GLORIOUS VICTORY

The game ends at the end of the fifth battle round.

The Nighthaunt player wins a **major victory** if they control both siege targets at the end of the game (see right). The Defender wins a **major victory** if the Nighthaunt player controls neither siege target. Any other result is a draw.

CONTROLLING SIEGE TARGETS

The siege targets in the Defender's territories are controlled by the last player to have any models within 1" of the terrain feature. If both players have any models within 1" of a siege target terrain feature, it is controlled by the Defender.

PATH TO GLORY

Path to Glory campaigns centre around collecting and fighting battles with a warband in the Age of Sigmar. Champions fight each other and gather followers to join them in their quest for glory, taking advantage of this age of unending battle to win glory and renown.

In order to take part in a Path to Glory campaign, you will need two or more players. All players will need to have at least one **HERO**, who is their champion, and must then create a warband to follow and fight beside their champion during the campaign.

The players fight battles against each other using the warbands they have created. The results of these battles will gain their warband favour. The warband will swell in numbers as more warriors flock to their banner, while existing troops become more powerful.

After gaining enough favour or growing your warband enough to dominate all others through sheer weight of numbers, you will be granted a final test. Succeed, and your glory will be affirmed for all time, and you will be crowned as the victor of the campaign.

CREATING A WARBAND

When creating a Path to Glory warband, do not select your army in the normal manner. Instead, your army consists of a mighty champion battling to earn the favour of the gods, and their entire band of loyal followers. As you wage war against other warbands, your own warband will grow, and existing units will become grizzled veterans.

WARBAND ROSTER

The details and progress of each warband need to be recorded on a warband roster, which you can download for free from games-workshop.com.

To create a warband, simply follow these steps and record the results on your warband roster:

1. First, pick an allegiance for your warband. Each allegiance has its own set of warband tables that are used to generate the units in the warband and the rewards they can receive for fighting battles. The warband tables included in this battletome let you collect a warband with the Nighthaunt allegiance, but other Warhammer Age of Sigmar publications include warband tables to let you collect other warbands from the Grand Alliances of Order, Chaos, Death and Destruction.

2. Next, choose your warband's champion by selecting one of the options from your allegiance's champion table. The champion you choose will determine the number of followers in your warband. Give your champion a suitably grand name, and write this down on your warband roster.

3. Having picked your champion, the next step is to generate your starting followers. These can be chosen from the followers tables for your allegiance. If your allegiance has more than one followers table you can freely choose which ones you use, selecting all of your followers from a single table or from several. Instead of choosing, you can place your destiny in the hands of fate and roll on the followers tables instead. To make a followers roll, pick a column from one of the followers tables and then roll a dice.

4. Your followers need to be organised into units. The followers table tells you how many models the unit has. Follower units cannot include additional models, but they can otherwise take any options listed on their warscroll. Record all of the information about your followers on your warband roster.

5. Instead of generating a unit of followers, your champion can start the campaign with a Champion's Reward, or one of your units can start with a Follower's Reward. No champion or unit can start the Path to Glory campaign with more than one reward each.

6. Finally, give your warband a name, one that will inspire respect and dread in your rivals. Your warband is now complete, and you can fight your first battle. Good luck!

TO WAR!

Having created a warband, you can now fight battles with it against other warbands taking part in the campaign. You can fight battles as and when you wish, and can use any of the battleplans available for Warhammer Age of Sigmar. There are some battleplans, for example in the *General's Handbook*, that have been designed specifically for use in Path to Glory campaigns.

The units you use for a game must be those on your roster. Units can either be fielded at their full roster strength, or broken down into smaller units, as long as no unit is smaller than the minimum size shown on its warscroll.

Any casualties suffered by a warband are assumed to have been replaced in time for its next battle. If your champion is slain in a battle, it is assumed that they were merely injured, and they are back to full strength for your next game, thirsty for vengeance!

GAINING GLORY

All of the players in the campaign are vying for glory. The amount of glory they have received is represented by the Glory Points that the warband has accumulated. Glory can be increased by fighting and winning battles, as described next. As a warband's glory increases, it will also attract additional followers, and a warband's champion may be granted rewards.

Warbands receive Glory Points after a battle is complete. If the warband drew or lost the battle, it receives 1 Glory Point. If it won the battle, it receives D3 Glory Points (re-roll a result of 1 if it won a major victory).

Add the Glory Points you scored to the total recorded on your roster. Once you have won 10 Glory Points, you will have a chance to win the campaign, as described below.

REWARDS OF BATTLE

Each allegiance has its own set of rewards tables. After each battle you can take one of the three following options. Alternatively, roll a D3 to determine which option to take:

D3 Option

1 **Additional Followers:** More followers flock to your banner. Either select a new unit or roll for a random one from a follower table, then add it to your warband roster. You can choose from any of your own follower tables, or from any of the follower tables from an allied warband table i.e. a warband table whose allegiance is from the same Grand Alliance as your own. In either case, if you wish to add a unit from a follower table that requires more than '1 roll', you must also reduce your Glory Points total by 1 (if you do not have enough Glory Points, you cannot choose a unit from such a table). Once 5 new units have joined your warband, you will have a chance to win the campaign, as described below.

2 **Champion's Reward:** Your champion's prowess grows. Roll on your allegiance's champion rewards table. Note the result on your warband roster. If you roll a result the champion has already received, roll again until you get a different result.

3 **Follower's Reward:** Your warriors become renowned for mighty deeds. Pick a unit of followers (not one from an allied warband table), then roll on your allegiance's followers rewards table. Note the result on your warband roster. If you roll a result the unit has already received, roll again until you get a different result.

ETERNAL GLORY

There are two ways to win a Path to Glory campaign; either by Blood or by Might. To win by Blood your warband must first have 10 Glory Points. To win by Might your warband must have at least 5 additional units of followers. In either case, you must then fight and win one more battle to win the campaign. If the next battle you fight is tied or lost, you do not receive any Glory Points – just keep on fighting battles until you either win the campaign… or another player wins first!

You can shorten or lengthen a campaign by lowering or raising the number of Glory Points needed to win by Blood, or the numbers of extra units that must join it to win by Might. For example, for a shorter campaign, you could say that a warband only needs 5 Glory Points before the final fight, or for a longer one, say that 15 are needed.

NIGHTHAUNT WARBAND TABLES

Use the following tables to determine the champion that leads your warband, the followers that make up the units which fight at their side, and the rewards they can receive after battle.

CHAMPION TABLE

Champion	Followers
Spirit Torment*	3 units
Knight of Shrouds on Ethereal Steed	4 units
Knight of Shrouds	4 units
Guardian of Souls with Nightmare Lantern	4 units
Lord Executioner	4 units

* *You receive a unit of 2 Chainghasts in addition to the Spirit Torment. The Spirit Torment is the warband's champion, and the unit of Chainghasts is a follower.*

RETINUE FOLLOWERS TABLE

D6	Followers
1-2	10 Chainrasps
3-4	3 Spirit Hosts
5	5 Glaivewraith Stalkers
6	4 Myrmourn Banshees

ELITE RETINUE FOLLOWERS TABLE
(uses 2 rolls, or 1 roll and 1 Glory Point)

D6	Followers
1-2	10 Grimghast Reapers
3-4	5 Hexwraiths
5	10 Dreadscythe Harridans
6	10 Bladegheist Revenants

HERO FOLLOWERS TABLE

D6	Followers
1-2	Cairn Wraith
3-4	Dreadblade Harrow
5-6	Tomb Banshee

BLACK COACH FOLLOWERS TABLE
(uses 3 rolls, or 1 roll and 2 Glory Points)

D6	Followers
1-6	Black Coach

FOLLOWERS REWARDS TABLE

D6   Reward

1   **Ghastly:** *These spectres are so distorted by amethyst magic that they have become the stuff of darkest nightmare.*

Subtract 1 from the Bravery characteristic of enemy units while they are within 12" of this unit.

2   **Deadly:** *In life, the members of this unit were famed for their martial prowess. Although that time is long forgotten, the spirits still retain an innate sense of where and when to strike a foe.*

Re-roll hit rolls of 1 for attacks made by this unit.

3   **Cruel:** *This unit is so hate-filled and so steeped in malicious ways that they draw power from their own spite. Every blow they strike comes with an extra twist in order to inflict maximum pain upon their foes.*

Re-roll wound rolls of 1 for attacks made by this unit.

4   **Spectral Swiftness:** *These spirits move with an unnatural swiftness. They do not glide from point to point, but seem impossibly to appear closer in the blink of an eye.*

Add 2" to this unit's Move characteristic.

5   **Unnatural Resilience:** *This unit has mastered their phantasmal forms and can discorporate more than other wraiths, allowing enemy blades and arrows to pass harmlessly through them.*

Re-roll save rolls of 1 for attacks that target this unit.

6   **Ghostly Blades:** *The shimmering blades wielded by this unit have a strange, balefire glow. In spectral fashion they pass through enemy armour, yet into flesh they bite all too deeply.*

Improve the Rend characteristic of this unit's melee weapons by 1.

CHAMPION REWARDS TABLE

2D6 Reward

2 Nagash's Judgement: *Your champion's actions have drawn Nagash's gaze… and been found wanting. It is best not to raise the ire of the Great Necromancer.*

You lose 1 Glory Point. In addition, your champion cannot gain any further rewards for the rest of the campaign.

3 Unnatural Swiftness: *Your champion has been gifted with supernatural speed, allowing them to glide effortlessly through the air at tremendous speed.*

Add 3" to your champion's Move characteristic.

4 Unholy Resilience: *Nagash has blessed this champion, granting its spectral form a will of spiteful adamant. This spiritual resilience allows it to fight on even past the point that other wraiths would have been torn apart.*

Add 1 to your champion's Wounds characteristic.

5 Otherworldly Miasma: *An ill-smelling grave-mist swirls about your champion. The cloying vapours makes targeting difficult, as the wraith slips into and out of the foetid atmosphere.*

Subtract 1 from hit rolls for attacks that target your champion.

6 Aspect of Terror: *This champion bears some unexpected aspect to its visage that unnerves a foe – perhaps a jaw that unhinges to impossible lengths, a deathly shriek that freezes marrow, or some terrifying visage concealed beneath a cloak.*

Subtract 1 from the Bravery characteristic of enemy units while they are within 6" of your champion.

7 Murderer's Legacy: *In life this spectre was a killer of extraordinary prowess, and such skills have carried over to the afterlife.*

Add 1 to wound rolls for attacks made by your champion.

8 Baleful Presence: *To be near this champion is to know fear, for panic and dismay wash outwards from this wraith in chilling waves of energy.*

Subtract 1 from casting rolls and charge rolls for enemy units while they are within 12" of your champion.

9 Touch of Death: *So full of pent-up malice is this champion that a mere touch from it is sometimes enough to stop a beating heart.*

Each time you make an unmodified hit roll of 6 for an attack made with your champion's melee weapons, that attack inflicts a number of mortal wounds equal to that weapon's Damage characteristic and the attack sequence ends (do not make a wound or save roll).

10 Ephemeral Form: *With the ability to phase into and out of the material world, this champion is notoriously difficult to strike.*

Subtract 1 from wound rolls for attacks that target your champion.

11 Infernal Gaze: *A single look from this champion is so horrifying that it can freeze the blood of any onlooker that dares to meet its gaze.*

In your hero phase, pick an enemy unit within 8" of your champion and roll 2D6. If the roll is greater than that unit's Bravery characteristic, it suffers D3 mortal wounds.

12 Siphon Soul: *This champion has been blessed by necromantic magics so that its weapon can suck the soul out of a wounded foe and transfer its energy. So does this wraith kill to make itself stronger.*

When your champion fights, if they inflict any wounds with their melee weapons, you can heal 1 wound allocated to your champion after all of the champion's attacks have been made.

WARSCROLLS

This section includes Nighthaunt warscrolls, warscroll battalions and endless spell warscrolls. Updated July 2018; the warscrolls printed here take precedence over any warscrolls with an earlier publication date or no publication date.

WARSCROLL BATTALION
NIGHTHAUNT PROCESSION

The vanguard of the Soul Wars, the Nighthaunts press forward relentlessly. To a mortal, the approach of a Nighthaunt army is a terrifying sight. However, to Nagash the procession is as he himself has ordained – an ordered affair of minions driven forward by the malign willpower of the more powerful spirits amongst them.

ORGANISATION

A Nighthaunt Procession consists of the following warscroll battalions:

- 1 Shroudguard

- 6 warscroll battalions chosen in any combination from the following list:
  - The Condemned
  - Chainguard
  - Execution Horde
  - Deathriders
  - Death Stalkers
  - Shrieker Host

ABILITIES

Bound Beneath Indomitable Will: *When a Nighthaunt procession gathers in full force, the amethyst magic of Shyish hangs heavy in the air. The spectral commanders that lead this dread army of gheists to war serve as beacons of this deathly energy, empowering their minions with an unholy resilience.*

Roll a dice each time you allocate a wound or mortal wound to a friendly **NIGHTHAUNT** model from this battalion within 12" of your general or a friendly **NIGHTHAUNT HERO** from the battalion. On a 6+ the wound is negated. If this battalion is part of a Nighthaunt army, this ability replaces the Deathless Spirits battle trait for all units in this battalion.

WARSCROLL BATTALION
SHROUDGUARD

When the whirling Bladegheist Revenants undertake the fell ritual of the Shroudguard they bond to the fell champion Nagash has chosen as their new master. In such a state they become a formidable bodyguard that will fight on even after absorbing blows that would normally destroy their supernatural forms.

ORGANISATION

A Shroudguard consists of the following units:

- 1 Knight of Shrouds or Reikenor the Grimhailer

- 2 units of Bladegheist Revenants

ABILITIES

Frenzied Fervour: *The Bladegheists of the Shroudguard are cursed with fanatical devotion to their spectral lord, and are incredibly hard to destroy in his presence.*

Roll a dice each time you allocate a wound or mortal wound to a **BLADEGHEIST REVENANT** model from a unit in this battalion wholly within 12" of a **KNIGHT OF SHROUDS** or **REIKENOR THE GRIMHAILER** from the same battalion. On a 5+, that wound or mortal wound is negated. If you use this ability, you cannot also use the Deathless Spirits battle trait to try to negate the same wound or mortal wound.

WARSCROLL BATTALION

DEATHRIDERS

When the spectral cavalry of the Nighthaunt processions amass alongside a Black Coach, they create a swell of supernatural energies. The speartip of the Nighthaut processions, the surging tide of Deathriders charge with unnatural speed to scythe down any foe foolish enough to stand before them.

ORGANISATION

A Deathriders battalion consists of the following units:

- 1-2 Dreadblade Harrows

- 2 units of Hexwraiths

- 1 Black Coach

ABILITIES

Spectral Spearhead: *Deathriders lead the Nighthaunt processions from the front, scything through their petrified prey before they can even react to the murderous spectral cavalrymen in their midst.*

Add 1 to charge rolls for units from this battalion. In addition, if you make an unmodified charge roll of 9+ for a unit from this battalion, it can fight immediately after you complete the charge move. This does not stop the unit from being picked to fight in the combat phase of the same turn. If this battalion is part of a Nighthaunt army, this ability replaces the Wave of Terror battle trait for all units in this battalion.

WARSCROLL BATTALION
THE CONDEMNED

The concentrated energies of massed Chainrasps awaken a depthless cruelty in their punishers. Thus are the Condemned goaded and compelled to heave forward and smite the foe. With the desperate fervour of their attacks, these battalions often lead assaults or are assigned to especially forlorn hopes.

ORGANISATION

The Condemned consists of the following units:

- 1 Spirit Torment
- 1 unit of Chainghasts
- 2 Chainrasp Hordes*

* Each Chainrasp Horde must contain at least 20 models.

ABILITIES

Cruel Taskmasters: *The spectral overseers of the Condemned push their tormented charges hard, never letting up whilst there are living foes yet to slay.*

You can re-roll failed hit rolls for attacks made by **CHAINRASP HORDE** units from this battalion while they are wholly within 15" of this battalion's **SPIRIT TORMENT** or **CHAINGHASTS**.

WARSCROLL BATTALION
CHAINGUARD

For many Nighthaunt processions the Chainguard form the centre of their assault – a mainstay formation around which the rest of the army manoeuvres. While the foe is pinned in place fighting the ever-returning Chainrasp Hordes, a wise spectral commander can ensure they seize the initiative with any number of counter-attacks.

ORGANISATION

A Chainguard battalion consists of the following units:

- 1 Guardian of Souls

- 2 Chainrasp Hordes*

* Each Chainrasp Horde must contain at least 20 models.

ABILITIES

The Heart of the Horde: *The cursed souls of the Chainguard are eternally bound to the will of the Guardian of Souls that accompanies them, and are drawn inexorably to the magic he wields.*

Each time a **Chainrasp Horde** from this battalion is affected by a Spectral Lure or Temporal Translocation spell cast by this battalion's **Guardian of Souls**, you can return D6 slain models to that unit (in addition to any models returned to the unit by the Spectral Lure spell).

WARSCROLL BATTALION
EXECUTION HORDE

When an Execution Horde is summoned, a Lord Executioner is surrounded by Spirit Hosts composed of the massed and intermingled souls of those whom he slew in life. The Nighthaunts use such small but hard-hitting battalions to supplement their fighting strength, often working alongside the massed Chainguard.

ORGANISATION

An Execution Horde consists of the following units:

- 1 Lord Executioner

- 3 units of Spirit Hosts

ABILITIES

The Headsman's Masses: *The spirit swarms that accompany an Execution Horde's master serve to distract his prey whilst he delivers the killing blow.*

Subtract 1 from hit rolls for attacks that target this battalion's **LORD EXECUTIONER** while a **SPIRIT HOST** unit from this battalion is within 6" of the attacker's unit. In addition, add 1 to hit rolls for attacks made by this battalion's **LORD EXECUTIONER** while any **SPIRIT HOST** units from this battalion are within 6" of the target unit.

WARSCROLL BATTALION
DEATH STALKERS

They are bringers of death, finality made manifest. Led by the driving and murderous passion of a Cairn Wraith, Death Stalkers are spectral killers that relentlessly hunt down the enemy whose name has been whispered to them in darksome rites. They fall upon the named foe with a nigh-unstoppable vengeful zeal.

ORGANISATION

A Death Stalkers battalion consists of the following units:

- 1 Cairn Wraith
- 2 units of Grimghast Reapers
- 2 units of Glaivewraith Stalkers

ABILITIES

Soul-marked Prey: *When Nagash desires the death of a certain target, he sends forth his Death Stalkers, who will fight with terrible and relentless purpose to see the subject of their master's ire slain.*

After set-up is complete but before the battle begins, pick one enemy unit to be soul-marked by this battalion. Add 1 to hit and wound rolls for attacks made by units from this battalion that target the soul-marked unit.

WARSCROLL BATTALION
SHRIEKER HOST

The scream of a single Tomb Banshee can kill even the mightiest warrior. When backed by a screeching hell-choir of Myrmourn Banshees and Dreadscythe Harridans, that shrieking builds to an unholy cacophony – an unnatural sound that often serves to break opposing forces already beset by the horror of a Nighthaunt procession.

ORGANISATION

A Shrieker Host consists of the following units:

- 1 Tomb Banshee

- 2 units of Dreadscythe Harridans

- 2 units of Myrmourn Banshees

ABILITIES

Mournful Wailing: *The wailing of so many tormented souls is enough to fill even the most disciplined heart with melancholy.*

Re-roll battleshock rolls of 1 for enemy units that are within 6" of any units from this battalion at the start of the battleshock phase. In addition, the Inspiring Presence command ability cannot be used on enemy units that are within 6" of any units from this battalion.

LADY OLYNDER
MORTARCH OF GRIEF

	MOVE	
WOUNDS	6"	SAVE
72	7 ✕ 4+	
	10	
	BRAVERY	

Lady Olynder is despair given form. She exudes hopelessness and casts an enfeebling gloom upon her foes. Accompanied by banshee handmaidens, the Mortarch of Grief bears the life-taking Staff of Midnight and horrors unknown beneath her veil.

MELEE WEAPONS	Range	Attacks	To Hit	To Wound	Rend	Damage
Staff of Midnight	2"	3	3+	3+	-2	D3
Banshee Handmaidens' Spectral Claws	1"	6	4+	4+	-	1

DESCRIPTION

Lady Olynder is a named character that is a single model. She is armed with the Staff of Midnight.

COMPANIONS: Lady Olynder is accompanied by two Banshee Handmaidens, who are armed with Spectral Claws. For rules purposes, the Banshee Handmaidens are treated in the same manner as a mount.

FLY: This model can fly.

ABILITIES

Ethereal: *Creatures whose bodies have rotted away are difficult to harm with ordinary weapons.*

Ignore modifiers (positive or negative) when making save rolls for attacks that target this model.

Frightful Touch: *With but a single, bone-chilling touch of their spectral claws, the banshee handmaidens can still a beating heart.*

If the unmodified hit roll for an attack made with the Banshee Handmaidens' Spectral Claws is 6, that attack inflicts 1 mortal wound and the attack sequence ends (do not make a wound or save roll).

Grave-sands of Time: *Lady Olynder's handmaidens bear gifts from Nagash, including a Grave-sand Hourglass through which mortal life itself slips.*

Once per battle, in your hero phase, you can choose either to inflict D6 mortal wounds on an enemy **HERO** within 6" of this model, or heal D6 wounds that have been allocated to this model.

Lifting the Veil: *Those that see what lies beneath Lady Olynder's veil die with deathmask expressions of shock and horror frozen upon their faces – their dying grief serving only to feed the Mortarch's insatiable desire.*

At the start of your hero phase, pick an enemy unit within 12" of this model that is visible to her and roll a dice. On a 1, nothing happens. On a 2+, that unit suffers a number of mortal wounds equal to the roll. In addition, if any enemy models are slain by this ability, immediately heal D3 wounds that have been allocated to this model.

Mortarch of Grief: *Chosen by Nagash to serve as his Mortarch of Grief, Lady Olynder's very presence serves as a psychological weapon of terrible potency.*

Add 1 to the number of models that flee from enemy units that fail a battleshock test while they are within 12" of this model.

Wail of the Damned: *The Handmaidens can loose a soul-piercing shriek that contains within its harrowing notes all the woes of the realms.*

At the start of your shooting phase, roll 2D6 for each enemy unit within 10" of this model. If the roll for the unit is higher than its Bravery characteristic, it suffers D3 mortal wounds.

MAGIC

Lady Olynder is a **WIZARD**. She can attempt to cast two different spells in each of your hero phases, and attempt to unbind two spells in each enemy hero phase. She knows the Arcane Bolt, Mystic Shield and Grief-stricken spells.

Grief-stricken: *Lady Olynder's incantations can cause a pall of misery and utter desolation to descend upon her enemies, so that their limbs feel leaden and their very will to live is sapped.*

Grief-stricken has a casting value of 7. If successfully cast, pick an enemy unit that is within 18" of the caster and visible to them. Until your next hero phase, subtract 1 from hit rolls for attacks made by that unit and add 1 to hit rolls for attacks made with melee weapons that target that unit.

COMMAND ABILITIES

No Rest For the Wicked: *Should the spectral forms of her minions be banished or destroyed, Lady Olynder will wrench their souls back from the underworlds time and again until her will is done.*

You can use this command ability in your hero phase if this model is your general and is on the battlefield. If you do so, you can return 1 slain model to each friendly **SUMMONABLE NIGHTHAUNT** unit that is within 12" of a friendly model with this command ability.

KEYWORDS	DEATH, MALIGNANT, NIGHTHAUNT, HERO, WIZARD, MORTARCH, LADY OLYNDER

The Mortarch of Grief's stately advance is heralded by waves of clanking, wailing Chainrasps.

KURDOSS VALENTIAN
THE CRAVEN KING

MOVE	6"
WOUNDS	7
SAVE	4+
BRAVERY	10

74

The cold fury of Kurdoss Valentian is matched only by his bitterness. Cursed to sit upon a throne but never rule, the Craven King vents his anger by mercilessly smiting those his queen commands him to. Enemy leaders are targeted with especial bile.

MELEE WEAPONS	Range	Attacks	To Hit	To Wound	Rend	Damage
Sepulchral Sceptre	1"	5	3+	3+	-2	D3
Wraith Heralds' Spectral Claws	1"	6	4+	4+	-	1

DESCRIPTION

Kurdoss Valentian is a named character that is single model. He is armed with the Sepulchral Sceptre.

COMPANIONS: Kurdoss Valentian is accompanied by two Wraith Heralds, who are armed with Spectral Claws. For rules purposes, the Wraith Heralds are treated in the same manner as a mount.

FLY: This model can fly.

ABILITIES

Ethereal: *Creatures whose bodies have rotted away are difficult to harm with ordinary weapons.*

Ignore modifiers (positive or negative) when making save rolls for attacks that target this model.

Frightful Touch: *Gifted with the touch of the grave, a touch from the spectral claws of Kurdoss' wraith heralds can silence the most vibrant of hearts.*

If the unmodified hit roll for an attack made with the Wraith Heralds' Spectral Claws is 6, that attack inflicts 1 mortal wound and the attack sequence ends (do not make a wound or save roll).

If I Cannot Rule, None Shall Rule!: *In the presence of Kurdoss Valentian's all-consuming bitterness and the cruel malice of his heralds, the commands of enemy generals turn to dust in their mouths even as they issue them.*

At the start of the enemy hero phase, after the opposing player receives their command point for that turn, roll a dice. On a 5+, subtract 1 from the enemy player's command points, to a minimum of 0, and you receive 1 command point.

Soul-crushing Smite: *When backed by the full measure of Kurdoss Valentian's might and bitterness, the Sepulchral Sceptre can blast his victim's soul clean out of its body.*

If the unmodified wound roll for an attack made with the Sepulchral Sceptre is 6, that attack has a Damage characteristic of D6 instead of D3.

Suffer No Rival: *Never is the Craven King's bitterness more evident than when he lashes out at those he sees as rivals to his hollow power.*

You can re-roll failed hit rolls for attacks made with the Sepulchral Sceptre if the target is an enemy general.

KEYWORDS	DEATH, MALIGNANT, NIGHTHAUNT, HERO, KURDOSS VALENTIAN

	MOVE		
WOUNDS	**14"**	SAVE	
7		**4+**	
	10		
	BRAVERY		

REIKENOR THE GRIMHAILER

In life, Reikenor was a sorcerer-king, a champion that denied Nagash his rightful due. In death, he is a wraith-wizard, cursed to lead armies and reap souls in the name of the Great Necromancer for all eternity.

MELEE WEAPONS	Range	Attacks	To Hit	To Wound	Rend	Damage
Fellreaper	2"	4	4+	3+	-1	2
Ghostly Hooves and Teeth	1"	3	4+	4+	-	1

DESCRIPTION

Reikenor the Grimhailer is a named character that is a single model. He is armed with Fellreaper.

MOUNT: Reikenor the Grimhailer's mount, Kyllaron, attacks with Ghostly Hooves and Teeth.

FLY: This model can fly.

ABILITIES

Corpse Candles: *When Reikenor prepares to cast a spell by snuffing out the flame of a corpse candle, he can drain his own or a victim's essence to help fuel his sorcery.*

In your hero phase, before this model attempts to cast a spell, you can say that it will snuff out a corpse candle. If you do so, pick either this model or an enemy model within 12" of this model. That model suffers 1 mortal wound. If the mortal wound was suffered by an enemy model, add 1 to the casting roll; if the mortal wound was suffered by this model, add 3 to the casting roll.

Ethereal: *Creatures whose bodies have rotted away are difficult to harm with ordinary weapons.*

Ignore modifiers (positive or negative) when making save rolls for attacks that target this model.

Frightful Touch: *The wraith-touch of Reikenor is imbued with the pure finality of death, an unholy force that is transferred to the blade of the scythe Fellreaper. The weapon has a penchant for ghosting through flesh to still a beating heart.*

If the unmodified hit roll for an attack made with Fellreaper is 6, that attack inflicts 2 mortal wounds and the attack sequence ends (do not make a wound or save roll).

Reaped Like Corn: *Fellreaper can be swung in great sweeping arcs, cutting down whole ranks of enemy warriors.*

You can re-roll failed hit rolls for attacks made with Fellreaper if the target unit has 5 or more models.

MAGIC

Reikenor the Grimhailer is a **WIZARD**. He can attempt to cast one spell in your hero phase, and attempt to unbind one spell in the enemy hero phase. He knows the Arcane Bolt, Mystic Shield and Wraithstorm spells.

Wraithstorm: *Reikenor tears the souls from his victims and commands them to assail their allies.*

Wraithstorm has a casting value of 7. If successfully cast, pick an enemy unit within 12" of the caster that is visible to them. That unit suffers D3 mortal wounds. If any models in that unit are slain as a result of this spell, that unit immediately suffers an additional D3 mortal wounds.

KEYWORDS	DEATH, MALIGNANT, NIGHTHAUNT, HERO, WIZARD, REIKENOR THE GRIMHAILER

76

MOVE **6"**
WOUNDS **5**
SAVE **4+**
10
BRAVERY

KNIGHT OF SHROUDS

A Knight of Shrouds is a master tactician, and his commands inspire nearby spirits to greater heights of malicious fury. A deadly bladesman, the Knight wields a Sword of Stolen Hours, an enchanted weapon that increases his own power with each kill.

MELEE WEAPONS	Range	Attacks	To Hit	To Wound	Rend	Damage
Sword of Stolen Hours	1"	4	3+	3+	-1	2

DESCRIPTION

A Knight of Shrouds is a single model armed with a Sword of Stolen Hours.

FLY: This model can fly.

ABILITIES

Ethereal: *Creatures whose bodies have rotted away are difficult to harm with ordinary weapons.*

Ignore modifiers (positive or negative) when making save rolls for attacks that target this model.

Stolen Hours: *The bearer of a sword of stolen hours can steal vital energy from a foe and use it to increase their own power.*

Each time a wound inflicted by this model's Sword of Stolen Hours slays an enemy **HERO**, heal 1 wound allocated to this model.

COMMAND ABILITIES

Spectral Overseer: *In life, the Knight of Shrouds commanded legions of devoted soldiers. In death, he turns his military genius to the command of shrieking spirits and vengeful phantasms.*

You can use this command ability at the start of the combat phase. If you do so, pick a friendly model with this command ability. Add 1 to hit rolls for friendly **NIGHTHAUNT** units while they are wholly within 12" of that model in that combat phase.

KEYWORDS	DEATH, MALIGNANT, NIGHTHAUNT, HERO, KNIGHT OF SHROUDS

MOVE **12"**
WOUNDS **6**
SAVE **4+**
10
BRAVERY

KNIGHT OF SHROUDS
ON ETHEREAL STEED

On the bleakest nights of the human soul, the Knights of Shrouds ride at the head of a massed gathering of undead. Their disembodied voices ring out over the moans of the deceased even as they steal the lives from their foes.

MELEE WEAPONS	Range	Attacks	To Hit	To Wound	Rend	Damage
Sword of Stolen Hours	1"	4	3+	3+	-1	2
Ghostly Hooves and Teeth	1"	2	4+	5+	-	1

DESCRIPTION

A Knight of Shrouds on Ethereal Steed is a single model armed with a Sword of Stolen Hours.

MOUNT: This model's Ethereal Steed attacks with Ghostly Hooves and Teeth.

FLY: This model can fly.

ABILITIES

Ethereal: *Creatures whose bodies have rotted away are difficult to harm with ordinary weapons.*

Ignore modifiers (positive or negative) when making save rolls for attacks that target this model.

Stolen Hours: *The bearer of a sword of stolen hours can steal vital energy from a foe and use it to increase their own power.*

Allocate wounds inflicted by this model's Sword of Stolen Hours before allocating wounds inflicted by this model's Ghostly Hooves and Teeth. Each time a wound inflicted by this model's Sword of Stolen Hours slays an enemy **HERO**, heal 1 wound allocated to this model.

COMMAND ABILITIES

Lord of Gheists: *Each Knight of Shrouds was a mighty general in mortal life, and still retains the ability to spur their soldiery to great feats of arms.*

You can use this command ability at the start of the combat phase. If you do so, pick a friendly **NIGHTHAUNT** unit that is wholly within 18" of a friendly model with this command ability. Add 1 to the Attacks characteristic of that unit's melee weapons in that combat phase. A unit cannot benefit from this command ability more than once per phase.

KEYWORDS	DEATH, MALIGNANT, NIGHTHAUNT, HERO, KNIGHT OF SHROUDS

MOVE 6"

WOUNDS 5

SAVE 4+

BRAVERY 10

GUARDIAN OF SOULS
WITH NIGHTMARE LANTERN

A Guardian of Souls keeps vigil over the dead whilst driving those around them to the heights of malice. When one of these sorcerous spectres goes to war, hundreds of the living dead are drawn to their lantern's flame from leagues around.

MELEE WEAPONS	Range	Attacks	To Hit	To Wound	Rend	Damage
Chill Blade	1"	3	3+	3+	-1	1
Maul of Judgement	1"	2	3+	3+	-	2

DESCRIPTION

A Guardian of Souls with Nightmare Lantern is a single model armed with a Chill Blade or Maul of Judgement.

FLY: This model can fly.

ABILITIES

Ethereal: *Creatures whose bodies have rotted away are difficult to harm with ordinary weapons.*

Ignore modifiers (positive or negative) when making save rolls for attacks that target this model.

Nightmare Lantern: *The cursed light of Nagashizzar bound within a nightmare lantern invigorates the dark souls of any Nighthaunts it illuminates.*

Add 1 to wound rolls for attacks made with melee weapons used by friendly **NIGHTHAUNT** units that are wholly within 12" of this model.

MAGIC

This model is a **WIZARD**. It can attempt to cast one spell in your hero phase, and attempt to unbind one spell in the enemy hero phase. It knows the Arcane Bolt, Mystic Shield and Spectral Lure spells.

Spectral Lure: *Channelling the unholy light of his nightmare lantern, the Guardian summons forth the spirits of the dead.*

Spectral Lure has a casting value of 6. If successfully cast, pick a friendly **SUMMONABLE NIGHTHAUNT** unit wholly within 24" of the caster. You can either heal D6 wounds that have been allocated to that unit or, if no wounds have been allocated to the unit, you can return a number of slain models to it that have a combined Wounds characteristic equal to or less than the roll of a D6.

KEYWORDS	DEATH, MALIGNANT, NIGHTHAUNT, HERO, WIZARD, GUARDIAN OF SOULS

Using the fell fumes of a nightmare lantern, a Guardian of Souls summons the spirits of the long departed, further swelling the phantasmal ranks of the Nighthaunts.

• WARSCROLL •

SPIRIT TORMENT

The masked creatures known as Spirit Torments were pitiless jailers in life. In death they seek out those that Nagash deems his by right of rulership, bludgeoning them with their ensorcelled iron padlocks before locking away their souls.

MELEE WEAPONS	Range	Attacks	To Hit	To Wound	Rend	Damage
Shacklegheist Chains	2"	3	4+	3+	-2	D3

MOVE 6" · **WOUNDS** 5 · **SAVE** 4+ · **BRAVERY** 10

DESCRIPTION

A Spirit Torment is a single model. It is armed with Shacklegheist Chains.

FLY: This model can fly.

ABILITIES

Ethereal: *Creatures whose bodies have rotted away are difficult to harm with ordinary weapons.*

Ignore modifiers (positive or negative) when making save rolls for attacks that target this model.

Nagash's Bidding: *Spirit Torments ensure that Nagash's unrepentant hosts redouble their efforts to carry out his bidding.*

You can re-roll hit rolls of 1 for friendly **NIGHTHAUNT** units while they are wholly within 12" of any friendly **SPIRIT TORMENTS**.

Captured Soul Energy: *The chains and padlocks carried by Spirit Torments can capture the departing spirit of a slain foe.*

At the start of the battleshock phase, if 3 or more enemy models were slain that turn, pick a friendly **NIGHTHAUNT** unit within 6" of this model and heal D3 wounds that have been allocated to that unit. If 3 or more enemy

STORMCAST ETERNAL models were slain that turn, heal 3 wounds instead of D3 wounds.

Alternatively, instead of healing the unit you picked, if models from that unit have been slain, you can return them to the unit. Roll a D3; you can return any slain models to that unit that have a combined Wounds characteristic of less than or equal to the number you rolled.

If your army includes more than one **SPIRIT TORMENT**, at least 3 enemy models must have been slain during the turn for each **SPIRIT TORMENT** that uses this ability, and no **SPIRIT TORMENT** can use this ability more than once in the same battleshock phase.

KEYWORDS	DEATH, MALIGNANT, NIGHTHAUNT, HERO, SPIRIT TORMENT

• WARSCROLL •

CHAINGHASTS

Encased within their iron harness, it is a Chainghast's fate to remain imprisoned, eternally in thrall to Spirit Torments. They carry emotionally burdened ghastflails – heavy bludgeoning weights that cast bolts of pure misery when swung.

MISSILE WEAPONS	Range	Attacks	To Hit	To Wound	Rend	Damage
Ghastflails	15"	D3	4+	3+	-2	1
MELEE WEAPONS	**Range**	**Attacks**	**To Hit**	**To Wound**	**Rend**	**Damage**
Ghastflails	2"	See below	4+	3+	-1	1

MOVE 6" · **WOUNDS** 2 · **SAVE** 4+ · **BRAVERY** 10

DESCRIPTION

A unit of Chainghasts has any number of models, each armed with Ghastflails.

FLY: This unit can fly.

ABILITIES

Ethereal: *Creatures whose bodies have rotted away are difficult to harm with ordinary weapons.*

Ignore modifiers (positive or negative) when making save rolls for attacks that target this unit.

Another Link in the Chain: *Chainghasts act as conduits for Spirit Torments, ensuring all nearby Nighthaunts are invigorated by deathly energies.*

While this unit is wholly within 12" of a friendly **SPIRIT TORMENT**, you can re-roll hit rolls of 1 for friendly **NIGHTHAUNT** units while they are wholly within 12" of this unit.

Sweeping Blows: *With their heavy chains and weights, ghastflails batter anything they come in contact with, bludgeoning armour and cracking bones.*

The Attacks characteristic of the Ghastflails melee weapon is equal to the number of enemy models within 2" of the attacking model when the number of attacks made with the weapon is determined.

KEYWORDS	DEATH, MALIGNANT, NIGHTHAUNT, SUMMONABLE, CHAINGHASTS

DREADBLADE HARROW

79

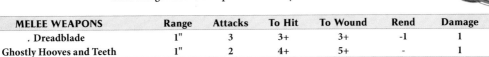

Dreadblade Harrows are spectral lieutenants, spirit knights mounted upon ghostly steeds. They are able to fade and reappear, so no place on the battlefield is safe from their charge and the sweep of their deadly dreadblades.

MELEE WEAPONS	Range	Attacks	To Hit	To Wound	Rend	Damage
. Dreadblade	1"	3	3+	3+	-1	1
Ghostly Hooves and Teeth	1"	2	4+	5+	-	1

DESCRIPTION

A Dreadblade Harrow is a single model armed with a Dreadblade.

MOUNT: This model's Ethereal Steed attacks with Ghostly Hooves and Teeth.

FLY: This model can fly.

ABILITIES

Phantasmal Discorporation: *Dreadblade Harrows are able to disappear in a spectral mist.*

If this model is more than 3" from any enemy models at the start of your movement phase, instead of making a normal move, you can remove it from the battlefield and then set it up anywhere on the battlefield more than 9" from any enemy models.

Dreadblade: *A Dreadblade can be wielded in a single hand to make a devastating thrust when the bearer charges a foe, or swung with two hands in deadly sweeping arcs once the bearer is engaged in combat.*

Add 1 to the Damage characteristic of this model's Dreadblade if it made a charge move in the same turn. Add 1 to the Attacks characteristic of this model's Dreadblade if it did not make a charge move in the same turn.

Ethereal: *Creatures whose bodies have rotted away are difficult to harm with ordinary weapons.*

Ignore modifiers (positive or negative) when making save rolls for attacks that target this model.

Curse of Loyalty: *In life these knights were retainers to one that would become a Knight of Shrouds. They failed to thwart his act of betrayal, and are now cursed to serve loyally beneath him.*

Re-roll wound rolls of 1 for attacks made with this model's Dreadblade while it is within 9" of a friendly **KNIGHT OF SHROUDS**.

KEYWORDS	DEATH, MALIGNANT, NIGHTHAUNT, HERO, DREADBLADE HARROW

LORD EXECUTIONER

To witness a Lord Executioner is to stare death in the face. Sent to claim the lives of those who have escaped the cold justice of Shyish, the spirits of the wrongfully executed drift around him, crying out their anguish into the night.

MELEE WEAPONS	Range	Attacks	To Hit	To Wound	Rend	Damage
Decapitating Greataxe	1"	3	3+	3+	-2	1

DESCRIPTION

A Lord Executioner is a single model armed with a Decapitating Greataxe.

FLY: This model can fly.

ABILITIES

Beheading Strike: *The cutting edge of a Lord Executioner's axe is razor-sharp, and they can use it to slice the head clean from a foe's body.*

If the unmodified wound roll for an attack made with a Decapitating Greataxe is 6, add 2 to the Damage characteristic of that weapon for that attack.

Ethereal: *Creatures whose bodies have rotted away are difficult to harm with ordinary weapons.*

Ignore modifiers (positive or negative) when making save rolls for attacks that target this model.

Staring Death in the Face: *The unwavering stare of a Lord Executioner seems to penetrate into the victim's very soul, filling them with bleak foreboding of their own demise.*

At the start of a combat phase, you can pick an enemy **HERO** within 3" of this model. Subtract 1 from hit rolls for attacks made by that **HERO** in that combat phase.

Disembodied Skulls: *The spirits that swirl around a Lord Executioner preserve his existence from threats.*

Roll a D6 each time you allocate a mortal wound to this model. On a 5+, the wound is negated.

KEYWORDS	DEATH, MALIGNANT, NIGHTHAUNT, HERO, LORD EXECUTIONER

TOMB BANSHEE

MOVE 6"
WOUNDS 4
SAVE 4+
BRAVERY 10

80

Tomb Banshees are apparitions of revenge who have long dwelt upon the dark deed that robbed them of vitality, love or contentment, becoming bitter and hate-filled. A single scream from a Tomb Banshee can freeze the life from even the bravest warrior.

MELEE WEAPONS	Range	Attacks	To Hit	To Wound	Rend	Damage
Chill Dagger	1"	1	4+	3+	-2	D3

DESCRIPTION

A Tomb Banshee is a single model armed with a Chill Dagger.

FLY: This model can fly.

ABILITIES

Ethereal: *Creatures whose bodies have rotted away are difficult to harm with ordinary weapons.*

Ignore modifiers (positive or negative) when making save rolls for attacks that target this model.

Frightful Touch: *The life-numbing touch of a Tomb Banshee can be enough to silence a beating heart, and that fell power channels through the creature's chill dagger.*

If the unmodified hit roll for an attack made with a Chill Dagger is 6, that attack inflicts D3 mortal wounds and the attack sequence ends (do not make a wound or save roll).

Ghostly Howl: *There is no describing the shrieking wail of the Banshee, as it is so horrific to hear that its sound alone can pierce the soul of any who hear it.*

At the start of your shooting phase, pick an enemy unit within 10" of this model and roll 2D6. If the roll is higher than the unit's Bravery characteristic, it suffers a number of mortal wounds equal to the difference between its Bravery characteristic and the roll.

KEYWORDS	DEATH, MALIGNANT, NIGHTHAUNT, HERO, TOMB BANSHEE

CAIRN WRAITH

MOVE 6"
WOUNDS 4
SAVE 4+
BRAVERY 10

The horrors known as Cairn Wraiths were once mass murderers or cruel executioners, mortals who developed such a taste for killing that upon death their unquiet spirits rose from the underworlds to continue their spree of terror.

MELEE WEAPONS	Range	Attacks	To Hit	To Wound	Rend	Damage
Reaper Scythe	2"	3	4+	3+	-1	2

DESCRIPTION

A Cairn Wraith is a single model. It is armed with a Reaper Scythe.

FLY: This model can fly.

ABILITIES

Ethereal: *Creatures whose bodies have rotted away are difficult to harm with ordinary weapons.*

Ignore modifiers (positive or negative) when making save rolls for attacks that target this model.

Frightful Touch: *The touch of a Cairn Wraith is imbued with the lethal chill of the grave, an unholy force that is transferred to the blade of its Reaper Scythe. Even the slightest nick from such a weapon might still a beating heart.*

If the unmodified hit roll for an attack made with a Reaper Scythe is 6, that attack inflicts 2 mortal wounds and the attack sequence ends (do not make a wound or save roll).

Reaped Like Corn: *The scythe wielded by a Cairn Wraith can be swung in great sweeping arcs, cutting down whole ranks of enemy warriors.*

You can re-roll failed hit rolls for attacks made with a Reaper Scythe if the target unit has 5 or more models.

KEYWORDS	DEATH, MALIGNANT, NIGHTHAUNT, HERO, CAIRN WRAITH

GLAIVEWRAITH STALKERS

A Glaivewraith Stalker is an unstoppable force. Its long blade always points at the beating heart of its intended victim. Though it drifts slowly toward its quarry, it is inevitable that the hunter's glaive will one day pierce the chest of its prey.

MELEE WEAPONS	Range	Attacks	To Hit	To Wound	Rend	Damage
Hunter's Glaive	2"	2	4+	3+	-	1

DESCRIPTION

A unit of Glaivewraith Stalkers has any number of models, each armed with a Hunter's Glaive.

DEATHBEAT DRUMMER: Models in this unit can be Deathbeat Drummers. A unit that includes any Deathbeat Drummers can retreat and charge in the same turn.

FLY: This unit can fly.

ABILITIES

The Point of Death: *The Hunter's Glaives wielded by these long-dead warriors always point compass-like towards their next victim, striking deep and true when hunter and prey come together.*

You can re-roll failed hit rolls for attacks made with this unit's Hunter's Glaives if this unit or the target unit made a charge move in the same turn.

Ethereal: *Creatures whose bodies have rotted away are difficult to harm with ordinary weapons.*

Ignore modifiers (positive or negative) when making save rolls for attacks that target this unit.

KEYWORDS	DEATH, MALIGNANT, NIGHTHAUNT, SUMMONABLE, GLAIVEWRAITH STALKERS

GRIMGHAST REAPERS

Arch plotters and schemers in life, Grimghast Reapers are cursed in their undeath to kill indiscriminately. Those foolish enough to stand before a Grimghast Reaper usually end their lives hacked apart into bleeding chunks of meat.

MELEE WEAPONS	Range	Attacks	To Hit	To Wound	Rend	Damage
Slasher Scythe	2"	2	4+	3+	-1	1
Death Knell	2"	1	3+	3+	-1	2

DESCRIPTION

A unit of Grimghast Reapers has any number of models, each armed with a Slasher Scythe.

EXTOLLER OF SHYISH: The leader of this unit is an Extoller of Shyish. An Extoller of Shyish is armed with a Death Knell instead of a Slasher Scythe.

FLY: This unit can fly.

ABILITIES

Ethereal: *Creatures whose bodies have rotted away are difficult to harm with ordinary weapons.*

Ignore modifiers (positive or negative) when making save rolls for attacks that target this unit.

Reaped Like Corn: *The scythes wielded by these ghostly warriors can be swung in great sweeping arcs, cutting down whole ranks of enemy warriors.*

You can re-roll failed hit rolls for attacks made with this unit's Slasher Scythes if the target unit has 5 or more models.

For Whom the Bell Tolls: *A Death Knell steals the life-force of those that it batters to death, and redirects it to harm any enemy creatures that are nearby.*

Allocate wounds inflicted by a Death Knell after allocating wounds inflicted by Slasher Scythes. For each enemy model that is slain by wounds inflicted by a Death Knell, you can inflict 1 mortal wound on an enemy unit within 3" of the model armed with the Death Knell.

KEYWORDS	DEATH, MALIGNANT, NIGHTHAUNT, SUMMONABLE, GRIMGHAST REAPERS

MOVE	6"
WOUNDS	1
SAVE	5+
BRAVERY	6

CHAINRASP HORDE

A horde of Chainrasps is a frightening force. A sword or axe might pass right through a Chainrasp without finding purchase, but the spiked clubs and rusted blades wielded by these evil beings can mangle flesh and shatter bone.

MELEE WEAPONS	Range	Attacks	To Hit	To Wound	Rend	Damage
Malignant Weapon	1"	2	4+	4+	-	1

DESCRIPTION

A Chainrasp Horde has any number of models, each armed with a Malignant Weapon.

DREADWARDEN: The leader of this unit is a Dreadwarden. Add 1 to the Attacks characteristic of a Dreadwarden's Malignant Weapon. In addition, a Chainrasp Horde has a Bravery characteristic of 10 instead of 6 while it includes a Dreadwarden.

FLY: This unit can fly.

ABILITIES

Ethereal: *Creatures whose bodies have rotted away are difficult to harm with ordinary weapons.*

Ignore modifiers (positive or negative) when making save rolls for attacks that target this unit.

Chilling Horde: *When Chainrasps gather in sufficient strength, few can withstand their grave-cold touch.*

You can re-roll wound rolls of 1 for this unit while it has more than 10 models.

KEYWORDS	DEATH, MALIGNANT, NIGHTHAUNT, SUMMONABLE, CHAINRASP HORDE

MOVE	8"
WOUNDS	1
SAVE	4+
BRAVERY	10

BLADEGHEIST REVENANTS

Such is the curse of the Bladegheist Revenants that they fight with the frantic desperation of a drowning man attempting to reach the surface. Eternally trapped in the last moments of their lives, these spirits fight with an unmatched frenzy.

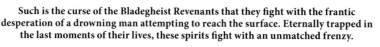

MELEE WEAPONS	Range	Attacks	To Hit	To Wound	Rend	Damage
Tomb Greatblade	1"	2	3+	3+	-1	1

DESCRIPTION

A unit of Bladegheist Revenants has any number of models. Each Bladegheist Revenant is armed with a Tomb Greatblade.

FLY: This unit can fly.

ABILITIES

Ethereal: *Creatures whose bodies have rotted away are difficult to harm with ordinary weapons.*

Ignore modifiers (positive or negative) when making save rolls for attacks that target this unit.

Fearful Frenzy: *Bladegheist Revenants share a collective, desperate frenzy that is exacerbated in the presence of those that, in their cursed madness, they perceive as their captors in life.*

You can re-roll failed hit rolls for attacks made by this unit if it is wholly within 12" of any friendly **SPIRIT TORMENTS** or **CHAINGHASTS**.

Whirling Death: *Twisting and whirling with deadly sweeps of their swords, the Bladegheist Revenants generate their own momentum, and can spin off in any direction at any time.*

This unit can retreat and charge in the same turn. In addition, add 1 to the Attacks characteristic of this unit's Tomb Greatblades if it made a charge move in the same turn.

KEYWORDS	DEATH, MALIGNANT, NIGHTHAUNT, SUMMONABLE, BLADEGHEIST REVENANTS

MYRMOURN BANSHEES

MOVE	8"	
WOUNDS	1	SAVE 4+
BRAVERY	10	

No enemy spell is safe from the diabolical hunger of the Myrmourn Banshees. They haunt the Mortal Realms in search of magic to consume and living foes to stab. Even the most potent of wizards is powerless before them.

MELEE WEAPONS	Range	Attacks	To Hit	To Wound	Rend	Damage
Chill Dagger	1"	1	4+	3+	-2	D3

DESCRIPTION

A unit of Myrmourn Banshees has any number of models, each armed with a Chill Dagger.

FLY: This unit can fly.

ABILITIES

Ethereal: *Creatures whose bodies have rotted away are difficult to harm with ordinary weapons.*

Ignore modifiers (positive or negative) when making save rolls for attacks that target this unit.

Spell-eaters: *These spirits were once wizards, but they failed to pay proper respect to Nagash, and are now cursed to agonisingly consume the magic of others.*

Once in each enemy hero phase, if this unit is within 18" of an enemy **WIZARD** that successfully casts a spell, this unit can attempt to unbind the spell in the same manner as a

WIZARD. If it does so, add 1 to the unbinding roll for every 4 models in this unit. In addition, if this unit unbinds an enemy spell, add 1 to the Attacks characteristic of this unit's Chill Daggers until the next enemy hero phase.

Once in each of your hero phases, if this unit is within 6" of an **ENDLESS SPELL**, this unit can attempt to dispel the endless spell in the same manner as a **WIZARD**. If this unit dispels an endless spell, it suffers D3 mortal wounds, but add 1 to the Attacks characteristic of this unit's Chill Daggers until your next hero phase.

KEYWORDS	DEATH, MALIGNANT, NIGHTHAUNT, SUMMONABLE, MYRMOURN BANSHEES

DREADSCYTHE HARRIDANS

MOVE	8"	
WOUNDS	1	SAVE 4+
BRAVERY	10	

In life they were healers, yet in spirit form they are cursed with the uncontrollable urge to kill, their hands morphed into scything instruments of slaughter. Shrieking as they swoop in for the attack, Dreadscythe Harridans crave only carnage.

MELEE WEAPONS	Range	Attacks	To Hit	To Wound	Rend	Damage
Scythed Limbs	1"	3	4+	3+	-1	1

DESCRIPTION

A unit of Dreadscythe Harridans has any number of models, each armed with Scythed Limbs.

SLASHER CRONE: The leader of this unit is a Slasher Crone. Add 1 to the Attacks characteristic of a Slasher Crone's Scythed Limbs.

FLY: This unit can fly.

ABILITIES

Ethereal: *Creatures whose bodies have rotted away are difficult to harm with ordinary weapons.*

Ignore modifiers (positive or negative) when making save rolls for attacks that target this unit.

Harrowing Shriek: *Even the bravest might quail upon hearing the unnerving shriek issued by the bloodthirsty Dreadscythe Harridans.*

Subtract 1 from hit rolls for attacks made by enemy models within 3" of this unit unless they have a Bravery characteristic of 6 or more.

Murderous Bloodlust: *The more blood that flows, the more aggressive the Dreadscythe Harridans become, recklessly slashing and stabbing in a flurry of violence.*

If the unmodified wound roll for an attack made with Scythed Limbs is 6, that attack has a Damage characteristic of 2 instead of 1.

KEYWORDS	DEATH, MALIGNANT, NIGHTHAUNT, SUMMONABLE, DREADSCYTHE HARRIDANS

SPIRIT HOSTS

MOVE	6"
WOUNDS	3
SAVE	4+
BRAVERY	10

84

Spirit Hosts are the souls of the damned, stripped of body and identity, screaming endlessly for the life they have lost. They long to take out their rage upon the living, and the very touch of their claws can turn blood to ice, or stop a heart from beating.

MELEE WEAPONS	Range	Attacks	To Hit	To Wound	Rend	Damage
Spectral Claws and Daggers	1"	6	5+	4+	-	1

DESCRIPTION

A unit of Spirit Hosts has any number of models, each armed with Spectral Claws and Daggers.

FLY: This unit can fly.

ABILITIES

Ethereal: *Creatures whose bodies have rotted away are difficult to harm with ordinary weapons.*

Ignore modifiers (positive or negative) when making save rolls for attacks that target this unit.

Frightful Touch: *Bearing the chill of an open grave, the spectral claws and daggers of the Spirit Hosts can still a beating heart with even the least of scratches.*

If the unmodified hit roll for an attack made with Spectral Claws and Daggers is 6, that attack inflicts 1 mortal wound and the attack sequence ends (do not make a wound or save roll).

KEYWORDS	DEATH, MALIGNANT, NIGHTHAUNT, SUMMONABLE, SPIRIT HOSTS

HEXWRAITHS

MOVE	12"
WOUNDS	2
SAVE	4+
BRAVERY	10

Upon ghostly steeds, the Hexwraiths ride straight through their foes, turning blood to ice and snatching souls from screaming warriors. Once knights both proud and cruel, these ethereal killers relive their glory by visiting pain and death upon mortals.

MELEE WEAPONS	Range	Attacks	To Hit	To Wound	Rend	Damage
Spectral Scythe	1"	2	4+	3+	-1	1
Hooves and Teeth	1"	2	4+	5+	-	1

DESCRIPTION

A unit of Hexwraiths has any number of models, each armed with a Spectral Scythe.

MOUNT: This unit's Skeletal Steeds attack with their Hooves and Teeth.

HELLWRAITH: The leader of this unit is a Hellwraith. Add 1 to the Attacks characteristic of a Hellwraith's Spectral Scythe.

FLY: This unit can fly.

ABILITIES

Ethereal: *Creatures whose bodies have rotted away are difficult to harm with ordinary weapons.*

Ignore modifiers (positive or negative) when making save rolls for attacks that target this unit.

Frightful Touch: *Even the slightest scratch from a Spectral Scythe can still a beating heart.*

If the unmodified hit roll for an attack made with a Spectral Scythe is 6, that attack inflicts 1 mortal wound and the attack sequence ends (do not make a wound or save roll).

Spectral Hunters: *As the Hexwraiths ride down their chosen prey, any whom they pass through en route to their target are subject to the phantasmal cavalry's life-leeching powers.*

In your movement phase, immediately after this unit has moved, you can pick an enemy unit that has any models that a model from this unit passed across. If you do so, roll a dice for each model from this unit that passed across the enemy unit. For each roll of 5+, that enemy unit suffers 1 mortal wound.

KEYWORDS	DEATH, MALIGNANT, NIGHTHAUNT, SUMMONABLE, HEXWRAITHS

BLACK COACH

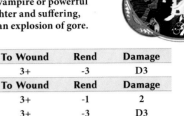

MOVE		
12	✦	4+ SAVE
WOUNDS		
	10	
	BRAVERY	

Driven by a Cairn Wraith and bearing the remains of a slain vampire or powerful Necromancer, the Black Coach seeks out sites of great slaughter and suffering, swelling with dark magic as it runs down helpless mortals in an explosion of gore.

MISSILE WEAPONS	Range	Attacks	To Hit	To Wound	Rend	Damage
Cairn Wraith's Soulreach Grasp	10"	1	3+	3+	-3	D3
MELEE WEAPONS	**Range**	**Attacks**	**To Hit**	**To Wound**	**Rend**	**Damage**
Cairn Wraith's Reaper Scythe	1"	3	4+	3+	-1	2
Cairn Wraith's Soulreach Grasp	3"	1	3+	3+	-3	D3
Relic Bearers' Spectral Claws	1"	✦	4+	4+	-1	1
Nightmares' Hooves and Teeth	1"	8	4+	4+	-	1

DAMAGE TABLE		
Wounds Suffered	**Move**	**Relic Bearers' Spectral Claws**
0-2	14"	9
3-4	12"	8
5-7	10"	7
8-9	8"	6
10+	6"	5

DESCRIPTION

A Black Coach is a single model driven by a Cairn Wraith armed with a Soulreach Grasp or a Reaper Scythe.

STEEDS AND CREW: The Black Coach is drawn by four Nightmares that attack with their Hooves and Teeth. Three Relic Bearers accompany the Black Coach, and can attack with their Spectral Claws. For rules purposes, the Nightmares and Relic Bearers are treated in the same manner as a mount.

FLY: This model can fly.

ABILITIES

Ethereal: *Creatures whose bodies have rotted away are difficult to harm with ordinary weapons.*

Ignore modifiers (positive or negative) when making save rolls for attacks that target this model.

Frightful Touch: *The icy touch of the Black Coach's Wraith crew is so fell and chill that a mere scratch from them can still a beating heart.*

If the unmodified hit roll for an attack made with the Cairn Wraith's Reaper Scythe is 6, that attack inflicts 2 mortal wounds and the attack sequence ends (do not make a wound or save roll).

In addition, if the unmodified hit roll for an attack made with the Relic Bearers' Spectral Claws is 6, that attack inflicts 1 mortal wound and the attack sequence ends (do not make a wound or save roll).

Evocation of Death: *The Black Coach absorbs death magic, swelling with power as it consumes more and more of that darksome force.*

At the start of each battle round, roll 3 dice for each **BLACK COACH** on the battlefield. For each 4+, that **BLACK COACH** gains a level of power. Levels of power are cumulative and last for the rest of the battle. They grant the following abilities:

First Level – Nimbus of Power: A supernatural glow emanates from the Black Coach, its fell touch invigorating the power within.

In your hero phase, heal D3 wounds that have been allocated to this model. In addition, at the start of your hero phase, pick 1 friendly **SUMMONABLE NIGHTHAUNT** unit wholly within 12" of this model and return D3 slain models to that unit. The returning models must be set up within 12" of this model.

Second Level – Unholy Vigour: Dark magic lends the vehicle unnatural speed and empowers its accompanying Nightmares and Wraiths to lash out with blurring swiftness.

Re-roll hit rolls of 1 for this model's melee weapons. In addition, this model can run and charge in the same turn.

Third Level – Spectral Scythes: These phantom blades look intangible but can slice flesh as easily as if forged from the finest steel.

After this model completes a charge move, pick an enemy unit within 1" of this model and roll a dice. On a 2+, that unit suffers D3 mortal wounds.

Fourth Level – Insubstantial Form: The Black Coach seems to flicker in and out of reality, making it all but impossible to trap and envelop.

This model can retreat and charge in the same turn.

Fifth Level – Witch-fire: Balefire crackles and arcs from the charging steeds and spinning wheels.

In your hero phase, roll a dice for each enemy unit within 3" of this model. On a 4+, that unit suffers D3 mortal wounds.

Reaped Like Corn: *The scythes wielded by these ghostly warriors can be swung in great sweeping arcs, cutting down whole ranks of enemy warriors.*

You can re-roll failed hit rolls for attacks made with this model's Reaper Scythe if the target unit has 5 or more models.

KEYWORDS	DEATH, MALIGNANT, NIGHTHAUNT, BLACK COACH

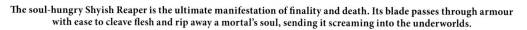

• ENDLESS SPELL WARSCROLL •

SHYISH REAPER

The soul-hungry Shyish Reaper is the ultimate manifestation of finality and death. Its blade passes through armour with ease to cleave flesh and rip away a mortal's soul, sending it screaming into the underworlds.

DESCRIPTION

Shyish Reaper is a single model.

Summon Shyish Reaper: *The wizard sweeps down their arm as they utter this spell's final incantation, and a fearsome scythe formed of purest amethyst magic tears through the wizard's foes with unstoppable force.*

Only **Nagash, Supreme Lord of the Undead** and **Nighthaunt Wizards** can attempt to cast Summon Shyish Reaper. It has a casting value of 7. If successfully cast, set up a Shyish Reaper model wholly within 6" of the caster.

PREDATORY: Shyish Reaper is a predatory endless spell. It can move up to 8" and can fly.

ABILITIES

Sweeping Death: *Once unleashed, a Shyish Reaper will carve through its prey, slicing through body and soul alike.*

When this model is set up, the player who set it up can immediately make a move with it.

Soul Reaper: *A Shyish Reaper is always on the hunt for souls, and can change direction without warning to sweep through its prey from an unexpected angle. Armour counts for naught against the deathly touch of the enchanted blade.*

Before moving a Shyish Reaper, pivot the model on the centre of its base so that it points lengthways in the direction you wish it to move. Then move it in a straight line in that direction. The initial pivot is free and does not count towards the distance the model moves.

After this model has moved, roll a dice for each model that it moved over (including models it moved over when it pivoted); if the roll is equal to or greater than the model's Save characteristic, that model's unit suffers 1 mortal wound.

Empowered by Shyish: *A Shyish Reaper's reach is that much greater when summoned within the realm of its namesake.*

If your battle is being fought in the Realm of Shyish, a Shyish Reaper can move 12" instead of 8".

KEYWORDS	ENDLESS SPELL, SHYISH, SHYISH REAPER

• ENDLESS SPELL WARSCROLL •

VAULT OF SOULS

This summoned chest siphons souls, filling itself to overflowing with the rich spirits of mortal-kind. Ever greedy for more, it eventually bursts, sending forth a lethal explosion of imprisoned souls to strike all those nearby.

DESCRIPTION

Vault of Souls is a single model.

Summon Vault of Souls: *At the wizard's command, a spectral casket takes shape, eager to feed upon the souls of the living.*

Only **Nagash, Supreme Lord of the Undead** and **Nighthaunt Wizards** can attempt to cast Summon Vault of Souls. It has a casting value of 6. If successfully cast, set up a Vault of Souls model wholly within 18" of the caster.

PREDATORY: Vault of Souls is a predatory endless spell. It can move 8" and can fly.

ABILITIES

Soul Siphon: *As the eerie Vault of Souls passes overhead, it draws the life-essence of those nearby into itself to lethal effect.*

After this model is set up or has moved, roll a dice for each model within 6" of it. On a 6+, that model's unit suffers 1 mortal wound.

Soul Eruption: *Should a Vault of Souls glut itself too greedily, the captured spirits within will burst free, tearing at those nearby in their desperation to escape.*

Keep track of the number of mortal wounds inflicted by this model. If the total is 20 or more at the end of any phase, all units within 6" of this model suffer D6 mortal wounds, and then this model is dispelled.

Empowered by Shyish: *Within the Realm of Death, it is even harder to escape the soul-siphoning reach of a Vault of Souls.*

If your battle is being fought in the Realm of Shyish, the range of this model's Soul Siphon ability is 9" instead of 6".

KEYWORDS	ENDLESS SPELL, SHYISH, VAULT OF SOULS

MORTALIS TERMINEXUS

The hourglass of fate known as the Mortalis Terminexus can speed the passage of time, aging those nearby to bones and dust in the blink of an eye, or it can be used to reverse the chronological order, restoring youth and vitality.

DESCRIPTION

Mortalis Terminexus is a single model.

Summon Mortalis Terminexus: *A spectral hourglass filled with shifting grave-sand takes shape, promising temporal grace or doom to mortal and immortal alike.*

Only **NAGASH, SUPREME LORD OF THE UNDEAD** and **NIGHTHAUNT WIZARDS** can attempt to cast Summon Mortalis Terminexus. It has a casting value of 6. If successfully cast, set up a Mortalis Terminexus model wholly within 18" of the caster.

PREDATORY: Mortalis Terminexus is a predatory endless spell. It can move 8" and can fly.

ABILITIES

Keeper of Mortality: *A Mortalis Terminexus holds the power of life and death within its shimmering form.*

After this model is set up or has moved, the controlling player must decide whether the Mortalis Terminexus will reverse or hasten time.

If they choose to reverse time, heal D3 wounds allocated to each unit within 6" of this model.

If they choose to hasten time, each unit within 6" of this model suffers D3 mortal wounds.

Empowered by Shyish: *The temporal dominion of a Mortalis Terminexus is greatly augmented within the Realm of Death.*

If your battle is being fought in the Realm of Shyish, the range of this model's Keeper of Mortality ability – whether the controlling player chose to reverse or hasten time – is 12" instead of 6".

KEYWORDS	ENDLESS SPELL, SHYISH, MORTALIS TERMINEXUS

Mortalis Terminexus, the Shyish Reaper and the Vault of Souls are brought forth by a Guardian of Souls, granting the blessings of the Realm of Death to the mortals who have earned his ire.

PITCHED BATTLE PROFILES

The table below provides points, minimum unit sizes and battlefield roles for the warscrolls and warscroll battalions in this book, for use in Pitched Battles. Spending the points listed on this table allows you to take a minimum-sized unit with any of its upgrades. Understrength units cost the full amount of points. Larger units are taken in multiples of their minimum unit size; multiply their cost by the same amount as you multiplied their size. If a unit has two points values separated by a slash (e.g. '60/200'), the second value is for a maximum-sized unit. Units that are listed as 'Unique' are named characters and can only be taken once in an army. A unit that has any of the keywords listed on the Allies table can be taken as an allied unit by a Nighthaunt army. Updated July 2018; the profiles printed here take precedence over any profiles with an earlier publication date or no publication date.

NIGHTHAUNT WARSCROLL	UNIT SIZE MIN	UNIT SIZE MAX	POINTS	BATTLEFIELD ROLE	NOTES
Chainrasp Horde	10	40	80/280	Battleline	
Cairn Wraith	1	1	60	Leader	
Dreadblade Harrow	1	1	100	Leader	
Guardian of Souls with Nightmare Lantern	1	1	140	Leader	
Knight of Shrouds	1	1	120	Leader	
Knight of Shrouds on Ethereal Steed	1	1	140	Leader	
Kurdoss Valentian, the Craven King	1	1	220	Leader	Unique
Lady Olynder, Mortarch of Grief	1	1	240	Leader	Unique
Lord Executioner	1	1	80	Leader	
Reikenor the Grimhailer	1	1	180	Leader	Unique
Spirit Torment	1	1	120	Leader	
Tomb Banshee	1	1	80	Leader	
Black Coach	1	1	280	Behemoth	
Bladegheist Revenants	5	20	90/320		
Chainghasts	2	4	80		
Dreadscythe Harridans	5	20	90/320		
Glaivewraith Stalkers	4	16	60		
Grimghast Reapers	10	30	140/360		Battleline in Nighthaunt army
Hexwraiths	5	20	160		Battleline in Nighthaunt army
Myrmourn Banshees	4	12	80/210		
Spirit Hosts	3	12	120		Battleline in Nighthaunt army
Chainguard	-	-	120	Warscroll Battalion	
The Condemned	-	-	150	Warscroll Battalion	
Death Stalkers	-	-	120	Warscroll Battalion	
Deathriders	-	-	130	Warscroll Battalion	
Execution Horde	-	-	100	Warscroll Battalion	
Nighthaunt Procession	-	-	80	Warscroll Battalion	
Shrieker Host	-	-	140	Warscroll Battalion	
Shroudguard	-	-	110	Warscroll Battalion	
Mortalis Terminexus	1	1	60	Endless Spell	
Shyish Reaper	1	1	40	Endless Spell	
Vault of Souls	1	1	40	Endless Spell	

DEATH	ALLIES
Nighthaunt	Deathlords, Soulblight